# Classic Porsche
## Racing Cars

By the same author

PORSCHE - DOUBLE WORLD CHAMPIONS
PORSCHE 911 AND DERIVATIVES
PORSCHE 911 TURBO
PORSCHE
PORSCHE STORY
PORSCHE PROGRESS

# Classic Porsche Racing Cars

Michael Cotton

Patrick Stephens Limited

First Published in 1988

British Library Cataloguing in Publication Data

Cotton, Michael, *1938–*
    Classic Porsche racing cars.
    1.  Porsche racing cars, 1951–1983
    I.  Title
    629.2'28

ISBN 1–85260–137–X

Patrick Stephens Limited is part of the Thorsons Publishing Group, Wellingborough, Northamptonshire, NN8 2RQ, England

Printed in Great Britain by the Bath Press, Avon

10  9  8  7  6  5  4  3  2

# Contents

# Foreword

By *Peter Falk*
Director of Competitions, Dr. Ing. h.c.F. Porsche AG

For four decades, Porsche has been building production sports cars which have come to be known on the roads of nearly all countries in the world. For almost 40 years, Porsche has sent its production sports cars and racing cars to compete on racing circuits worldwide. For Porsche, motoring has always been more than a mere tool for image enhancement: it has also, and in particular, served the purpose of speeding up the development of new automotive technologies and thus to fertilize series production.

Over the years, a multitude of racing cars have been developed, from the light, manoeuvrable hillclimb cars through the elongated Le Mans racers and long-legged rally cars to the big-displacement turbo-charged Can-Am Spyders. Each vehicle type has written its own small chapter in racing history, each type has gathered a 'fan club' of its own, both in-house and outside, and each type has had a more or less decisive influence on development trends in the racing and series sports car domains.

The reader of this book, which gives an impressive description of the development history of each individual vehicle type, will not only perceive Porsche's constant and strong commitment to racing sports car production and motoring as such, but also grasp some of the Porsche spirit motivating our designers, test engineers, mechanics and drivers and stimulating them to new achievements time and again.

# Author's introduction

The House of Porsche has a racing heritage matched only by that of Ferrari. While the Italian manufacturer has traditionally given his priority to Grand Prix racing, but produced marvellous sports racing cars until 1974, Porsche has been faithful to eudurance racing since 1951. Formula 1 was not ignored altogether though, for Dan Gurney won the 1962 French Grand Prix in a Porsche 804, and the Porsche-designed TAG V6 engine won Formula 1 titles in 1984, 1985 and 1986.

Through the development of Porsche's racing cars, mostly two-seaters, over a period of 36 years, one can learn much about the people who designed them. The rigours of 24-hour races, of 1,000 kilometre races at circuits such as the Targa Florio and the Nürburgring, make very special demands upon the machinery, calling for strength which runs counter to the quest for lightness. The combination of the two, of course, in correct proportion, is the secret of success.

The first 1,000 km test of any Porsche is not on a race track at all, but on a pavé section at Weissach. Thus, if any component is

*In the beginning ... the first major competition for a car wearing the Porsche badge, with factory support, was at Le Mans in 1951. The aluminium–bodied, Gmünd–origined 356 was driven by French importer Auguste Veuillet, partnered by Edmonde Mouche.*

too weak, it will fail there rather than in public. Porsche has an excellent reputation for strength and reliability, though no product has ever been described as heavy.

Throughout the 1950s Porsches were regular class-winners, sometimes nearing the front of the field towards the finish. In the 1960s some victories were won, notably in Sicily, and towards the end of that decade came cars that could win on every continent: the 908, followed by the 917, the magnificent Can-Am cars, then the 935, the 936, the 956 and the 962.

With the twelfth Le Mans victory secured in 1987, Porsche is now the most successful make ever to tackle the French classic. There have been 15 successes in the Daytona 24-Hours too, 11 in the Targa Florio, three in the Monte Carlo Rally, two in the Paris-Dakar 'Raid'... the list goes on and on.

The constant striving for success in every field that relates to the product range is Porsche's hallmark. Without Porsche, endurance competitions would have been much the poorer in recent decades, and we hope to introduce you to the Stuttgart company's heritage throughout this book.

Michael Cotton

Professor Ferdinand Porsche earned a formidable reputation in the 1920s and 1930s as a designer of racing cars (the Auto Union Grand Prix cars were his creations), but the first car to wear a Porsche badge was not constructed until 1948, at Gmünd in Austria. The competitions debut of the factory team's 356 model was at Le Mans in 1951, at the personal invitation of organizer Charles Faroux who guaranteed that the German team would be made welcome.

Two cars were entered for the race but both were damaged in the days before the race, and one good 356 was assembled from the parts. It was driven by the Porsche agent in France, Auguste Veuillet (once a motor cycle racer) with Edmonde Mouche. The car weighed 745 kg (1,639 lb) and was powered by a lightly tuned, 44 bhp flat-four Volkswagen engine of 1,086 cc; the top speed was exactly 100 mph (162 km/h). The rear wheels were covered to reduce drag, and the underside was faired for the same reason. The front bumper bar was left in place, as it was found to act as a spoiler and improve stability at speed.

The exercise was successful, the 356 covering 1,766 miles (2,943 km) in 24 hours to finish in twentieth place overall, and win the 1,100 cc class. A year later the same drivers repeated

*The Porsche 356 driven by Veuillet and Mouche at Le Mans in 1951 finished in twentieth place overall, and won the 1,100 cc class. It averaged 118.3 km/h (73.54 mph).*

their performance, winning the class in a similar aluminium–bodied 356 built in Gmünd (the production cars, built in Stuttgart from 1950 onwards, had steel bodies and were heavier).

Later in 1951 two aluminium 356s were entered for the arduous Liège-Rome-Liège rally, again very successfully. Paul von Guilleaume and Count von der Muhle finished in third place overall and won the 1,500 cc class, a month before the 1.5 litre engine was announced for production models; Porsche's PR and competitions manager Huschke von Hanstein and Petermax Muller finished second in the 1,100 cc class.

The following year Porsches achieved even more remarkable results in the Liège-Rome-Liège rally, which was won by Helmut Polensky in a 356 1,500 Coupé. Hans Herrmann was third, von Guilleaume fourth, Werner Engel was ninth and von Hanstein tenth, and having five Porsches in the top ten placings enhanced the make's reputation considerably.

As the aluminium-bodied Porsches grew weary, it became clear that a more specialized competitions car would be needed to keep ahead of the opposition. The type 550 was prepared for the 1953 season and one of its principal features was the positioning of the engine (type 528) ahead of the transmission (type 519). In this respect it resembled the prototype 356, which Professor Porsche had cautioned would be unsuitable for customers. All production Porsches have featured 'plus two' seating, to this day.

The 550 needed to make no compromises for children and baggage, being conceived for competitions, and had a special tubular ladder frame chassis designed by Hermann Ramelow, who had previously designed the Glöckler Porsche specials. The engine was a flat-four of 1,448 cc (80 x 74 mm), and was equipped with a Hirth roller bearing crankshaft and twin Solex 40 mm carburettors. The power output was rated at 79 bhp on gasoline, but 95 bhp on alcohol.

Handling was vastly improved by the new layout which also entailed turning the suspension around so that the flat, longitudinal arms were leading instead of trailing; the torsion bar suspensions were inside the rear cross tube, but the front suspension and steering were taken directly from the 356. The two prototypes had aluminium bodies by Weidenhausen, the first being an open roadster which weighed 550 kg (1,210 lb),

*Porsche's first purpose-built racing car was the type 550, two of which were prepared for Le Mans in 1953. Richard von Frankenberg and Paul Frère finished fifteenth and won the 1,500 cc class, and this car driven by Hans Herrmann and Helm Glockler, was sixteenth. Powered by pushrod flat-four engines developing 79 bhp, they were timed at 199 km/h (123 mph) on the Mulsanne straight.*

the second a coupé which weighed 590 kg (1,298 lb). The top speed was marginally over 200 km/h (125 mph).

The type 550 made its debut in the Eifel races at the Nürburgring in May 1953, where Helm Glöckler won the 1,500 cc sportscar class. A month later Glöckler and Hans Herrmann teamed up for Le Mans, Richard von Frankenburg and Paul Frère driving the second car; both were in coupé form, not so much for driver comfort but because the cars would be faster on the long straight. The speed and reliability of the cars was amazing, for they ran through to fifteenth and sixteenth places overall without problems. There were no other finishers in the 1,500 cc class, and von Frankenberg's car covered 2,070 miles (3,331 km), Herrmann's 2,069 miles (3,333 km). That's what you call consistent!

These two 'prototype' 550s continued their winning ways. Herrmann won the 1,500 cc sportscar race preceding the German Grand Prix, and a week later he won the Freiburg hillclimb. After a factory overhaul both cars were entered for the Carrera Panamericana, and the Guatemalan driver José Harrarte duly won his class. Finally, in January 1954 Jaroslav Juhan won the 1,500 cc class in the Buenos Aires 1,000 km race.

These successes were with the Volkswagen-derived engine, but for the 1954 season Dr Ferry Porsche had something more potent to offer. This was the Porsche-designed flat-four engine, type 547, which delivered a healthy 110 bhp at 7,800 rpm. It was designed from scratch by Dr Ernst Fuhrmann, who had previously worked on the Cisitalia Grand Prix engine, and by today's standards was extremely complex to build — the valve gear alone, with 14 bevel gears, comprised about 500 parts, and overhauls were reckoned to take 200 hours.

In 1954 the 'Fuhrmann' engine was state of the art, with twin camshafts on each bank driven by a countershaft, two horizontal and two vertical shafts; it had twin-plug ignition, twin Solex 40 mm carburettors, a double-sided radial cooling fan, and at the bottom end was the Hirth roller bearing crankshaft.

The chassis was a development of that for the original car, but the rear torsion bars were relocated to allow the flexible longitudinal rear suspension arms to trail, rather than lead, so that stability and cornering power was improved. The rear frame members passed over, rather than under the driveshafts, and one crossmember was demountable, to make the car easier to maintain. The aluminium bodies, open and coupé, were designed by Erwin Kommenda and built by Weinsberg.

Hans Herrmann gave the 550/547 a fine debut by finishing third overall in the 1954 Carrera Panamericana event, winning

the 1,500 cc class by miles, at an average speed close to 100 mph (160 km/h), followed closely by Juhan in the earliest customer car. Porsche's management responded by adopting the 'Carrera' name, reserving it for special cars designed for competitions.

With Porsche's master mechanic Herbert Linge as passenger, Herrmann drove to sixth place overall in the Mille Miglia, winning the 1,500 cc class, and the factory team then moved on to Le Mans. There, Paul Stasse and Belgian jazz band leader Johnny Claes won the 1,500 cc class finishing twelfth overall, and a special 1,100 cc version (with reduced bore dimensions) finished fourteenth and won its class in the hands of Arkus Duntov — Chevrolet's development chief, and designer of the Corvette, with Gustave Olivier.

No one could accuse the fledgling Porsche company of picking minor events. From Le Mans they went to the Reims 12-Hours where von Frankenberg and Polensky won the 1,500 cc class, finishing eighth overall, followed home by Olivier and Veuillet. The German Grand Prix supporting race was memorable too, the top four places in the 1,500 cc sportscar race being claimed by Hans Herrmann, Richard von Frankenberg, Helmut Polensky and Huschke von Hanstein.

*The Porsche type 550 was designed as a 'spyder' (open car), and is seen in original form before the start of the 1954 Carrera Panamericana. Hans Hermann is at the wheel, and finished third in the race.*

At Avus, the famous banked track in Berlin, von Frankenberg and Herrmann were first and second, averaging over 120 mph (193 km/h) and touching 145 mph (233 km/h) on the straights. The last major success recorded by the prototype cars was in the 1955 Mille Miglia, Wolfgang Seidler and Helm Glöckler winning the 1,500 cc class and finishing eighth overall.

The type 550/1500 RS Spyder was put into low-volume production at the end of 1954, and within a year some 85 cars were delivered to private customers. The series was almost a carbon copy of the prototypes, except that the bodies were manufactured by Wendler of Reutlingen, and the 'dry weight' (without oil or fuel) was in the region of 600 kg (1,320 lb). Outwardly the main difference was the fitment of wider rear wheels, 5.25 x 16.

Credit for the first attachable aerodynamic device, used widely from 1968 onwards, should be given to the Swiss engineer Michael May, who had an adjustable 'wing' over the cockpit for practice at the Nürburgring in 1956. Unfortunately the

scrutineers did not approve, and neither did the Porsche representative, so the wing was promptly banned. A pity, because May had recorded the fourth fastest time overall!

That is going ahead a bit, though. Four cars were entered for Le Mans in 1955, equipped with larger brakes, and as usual they ran like clockwork to fourth, fifth and sixth places overall, cleaning up in the 1,500 cc class. Two 1,100 cc coupés dominated the smaller class so it was a fine weekend for Porsche, though terribly marred by the accident involving Pierre Levegh's Mercedes, which claimed the lives of 82 spectators.

For the Avus race von Frankenberg's car was equipped with a modified type 547 engine developing 125 bhp, and the top speed was raised to 225 km/h (140 mph). He had a great duel with Edgar Barth, driving an EMW, which ended when the East German's car broke its throttle linkage, and von Frankenberg was then able to claim the German Sportscar Championship.

*Helm Glockler, sixth at Le Mans in 1955 (the race marred by the terrible accident involving Levegh's Mercedes) is powered by the Fuhrmann–designed type 547 four-cam engine, of 1,498 cc developing 110 bhp. Von Frankenberg's car won the Index of Performance.*

One of many claims to fame for the 550A was its outright victory in the 1956 Targa Florio, a trophy that Porsche coveted particularly. Although visually very similar to the 550 Spyder, the A version had an entirely new tubular spaceframe chassis designed by Leopold Schmid, and at 44 kg (97 lb) saved 16 kg (35 lb) compared with the previous 'ladder' chassis. With a lighter aluminium body, still by Wendler, the 550A's weight was reduced to 550 kg (1,120 lb).

Improvements were seen right through the car. The rear suspension, formerly swing axle, was replaced by a more forgiving low pivot design. A new baulk ring, five-speed gearbox was developed, and the engine, with Weber carburettors, gave an honest 130 bhp in 1,500 cc form. In 1956 the factory ran a 1,587 cc version which gave as much as 160 bhp, just touching the tantalizing 100 bhp/litre figure for the first time. Some 37 customer cars were built, most of them equipped with headrest fairings.

The debut of the 550A was as good as Dr Porsche hoped, Wolfgang von Trips/Umberto Maglioli finishing fourth overall at the Nürburgring and Herrmann/von Frankenberg sixth. The factory was so encouraged that it placed a late entry for the Targa Florio, and Umberto Maglioli was nominated to drive it single-handed. Eleven laps of the 44-mile course would be tiring at touring speed, but Maglioli was of the old school, and no doubt the 550A was delightful to drive, and he finished the race

*The Type 550A Spyder, developed in 1956, is pictured at the Solitude circuit outside Stuttgart. A steel tube spaceframe replaced the steel ladder frame, saving weight, and the swing axle rear suspension was superseded by a low pivot design.*

15 minutes ahead of the opposition. They did not even need to change the Continental tyres!

The Mayor of Stuttgart greeted the team home, and production stopped in the factory while Dr Porsche congratulated everyone concerned.

Buoyed up by this success the Germans looked forward to Le Mans, eager to snap up good placings once the race had taken its toll on the Jaguars, Ferraris and Aston Martins. Just for a change, though, ill fortune was shared fairly evenly; Jaguar lost two D-types early when Paul Frère shunted at the Esses, taking the Fairman/Wharton entry with him, and Porsche lost three of their four 550s — suspension damage, ignition failure and a collapsed piston were reasons for retirement, but vons Trips and Frankenberg kept the Stuttgart flag flying with fifth place overall, again easy winners of the 1,500 cc category.

The Mille Miglia was run for the last time in 1957, for in the aftermath of an accident claiming the lives of the Marquis de Portago, his co-driver and several spectators, even the car-crazy

*A coupé version of the type 550A was prepared for Le Mans in 1956. Richard von Frankenberg and Wolfgang von Trips finished fifth, winning the 1,500 cc class as usual.*

Italians realized that road racing was just too dangerous (a conclusion the French had reached 50 years previously). It was another event that Porsche enjoyed, even though their 1.5 litre cars could not reach the front, and in the last race Umberto Maglioli claimed fifth place, and yet another class win.

Approaching the 1957 season, Porsche was sad to lose the services of the amiable young German Wolfgang von Trips to Ferrari, but glad for him to have the opportunity to race in Formula 1 events. In sports cars, though, he was an opponent, and by a stroke of fortune the East German EMW company withdrew from competitions, making available Edgar Barth. Competitions manager Huschke von Hanstein lost no time in preparing for him a good programme of circuit and European Hillclimb Championship events, with great success. Barth and Umberto Maglioli were fourth overall at the Nürburgring, and won their class, in the type 550, and Barth and von Hanstein later claimed fifth overall in Venezuela.

Mention should be made of the 550 nicknamed 'Mickey Mouse', with its wheelbase reduced by 20 cm, and with a narrower track. It was designed for higher straight-line speeds but was difficult to handle, and was destroyed at the Avus by von Frankenberg in a spectacular accident. It was caused by a suspension breakage, and pitched the car over the banking and down into the car park; the driver was thrown clear and landed in a bush!

Midway through the 1957 season Porsche produced a successor to the 550, which was 20 kg (44 lb) lighter and dispensed, at last, with the torsion bar rear suspension. Instead, the type 718/1500 RSK had coil springs, radius rods and a Watts linkage, enabling the designers to throw away the low pivot swing axles. In 1959 wishbones were adopted for the rear suspension, allowing a softer and less skittish ride, and the 718 became 'racing car conventional' in its rear suspension layout.

At the front, though, torsion bars were retained, and at first the outer ends of the top torsion bars were higher than the inner ends, resembling the letter 'K' turned sideways. The engineer's parlance for the 'K' model was quickly adopted and retained, although the actual layout was changed before customer cars were built.

Type 718 it was, though, with a lighter form of extruded steel tubes forming the space frame, and the steering system jointed to facilitate the central steering wheel position needed for the Formula 2 version. Particular attention was paid to the bodywork which was nearly 5 in (13 cm) lower, and was extremely smooth and tapered at the front, even enclosing the headlamps behind Plexiglass.

Altogether 37 customer cars were built for the 1958 season, and the factory continued to enjoy considerable success. Since it was now realized that professional drivers of Formula 1 calibre were needed to get the best out of these cars (especially on the

*The Porsche type 718 RSK Spyder replaced the 550A in 1957, and here Umberto Maglioli is seen in the car at Le Mans (the car retired, damaged). The 718's spaceframe was lighter, and low drag was a priority. The vertical tail fins were used on fast circuits.*

**Right** *By 1958 power from the 4-cam engine had been raised to 142 bhp, and the Porsches were drawing closer to the race leaders. Jean Behra (pictured at the Nürburgring) finished second in the Targa Florio, with Scarlatti.*

**Below** *A fine sight! Three Porsche RSKs cross the line at Le Mans in third, fourth and fifth positions. Jean Behra and Hans Herrmann were third (No.29) using the newly–developed, 160 bhp version of the engine at 1,587 cc.*

fast tracks), Jean Behra was engaged as a works driver, and Stirling Moss was hired on a race-to-race basis. These two made a cracking start to the 1958 season, finishing third overall in Buenos Aires in January, behind two 3 litre Ferraris.

Harry Schell and Wolfgang Seidel followed up with third place overall at Sebring, then Behra and Giorgio Scarlatti drove superbly into second place in the Targa Florio, again beaten by a 3 litre Ferrari. The 1,587 cc version of this engine, developing 160 bhp, was raced for the first time at Le Mans where Behra and Herrmann ran home in third place overall, behind a Ferrari 250 TR and an Aston Martin DB3S, followed in fourth place by Barth and Frère, and fifth by Linge and Count Carel Godin de Beaufort.

With the latest wishbone rear suspension, Wolfgang von Trips (returning to Porsche for one season only) finished third with Jo Bonnier at Sebring in 1969, and later in the season finished a close second in the Tourist Trophy at Goodwood, putting

*Jean Behra, third at Le Mans in 1958, and Hans Herrmann (with cigarette) are congratulated by Herbert Linge who finished fifth.*

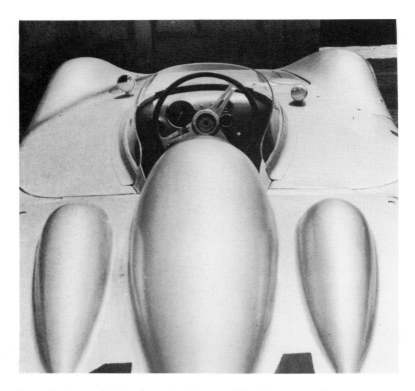

*Porsche's first foray into single-seater racing was the preparation of a Formula 2 car in 1957. It was almost identical to the type 718 RSK, but the driving seat was in the centre!*

Porsche into third place in the World Championship. Between these events, Edgar Barth and Wolfgang Seidel won the Targa Florio outright, this being Porsche's first-ever Manufacturer's Championship victory. The last event for that model, entered by the factory, was the Buenos Aires race in January 1960, where Jo Bonnier and Graham Hill raced to third place overall.

New regulations in 1960 required a full-width windscreen not less than 25 cm (10 in) in height, and Porsche felt that this called for new bodywork. The wheelbase was extended by 10 cm (4 in) to 220 cm (89 in), the bodywork was made wider, but the excellent design of the body meant that the top speed was impaired by no more than 100 rpm, or 4 km/h (2.5 mph). The chassis was very similar to the previous model's except that the rear frame was removable, and the drum brakes were increased in size and made more powerful.

A variety of engines was installed in four seasons including the 547/3 (1,498 cc, 150 bhp), the 547/4 (1,587 cc, 160 bhp and 1,606 cc, 160 bhp), 547/5 (1,679 cc, 170 bhp), and 587 (1,966 cc, plain bearings, 165 bhp). For one coupé only, early in 1962, the new flat-eight cylinder engine was installed, of 1,982 cc and developing 210 bhp, in a parallel programme with Formula 1.

With bodies by Wendler, the weight went back up to 550 kg (1,210 lb), most of the increase accounted for by the laminated glass windscreens, and most were in Spyder form; it is thought that 16 RS 60s were built, and 14 RS 61s.

The RS 60 made a stirring start to the season in Buenos Aires, where five of them claimed places in the top eight after 1,000 km of racing. Third overall, behind a pair of Ferraris, were Maglioli and Herrmann in a 1.6 litre model, and better was to come at

*Porsche's four-car team for Le Mans in 1960 comprised three type 718 RS 60 Spyders plus a 356B 1600 GS Carrera GTL Abarth (No.35).*

*The RS 60 model ran in spyder form at Le Mans, but with an elevated tail. This car, driven by Edgar Barth and Wolfgang Seidel, finished eleventh.*

Sebring where Olivier Gendebien and Herrmann were the outright winners ahead of Bob Holbert, Schlechter and Fowler in a 1500 ... and behind them were no fewer than six Ferraris!

On, then, to the Targa Florio, where Bonnier and Herrmann scored Porsche's third outright success on the island, ahead of von Trips and Phil Hill in a Ferrari Dino. At the Nürburgring a rather unexpected victory was taken by Moss and Gurney in a Maserati Tipo 61 ahead of Bonnier and Gendebien in an RS 60, and the short season concluded at Le Mans in June. Had Porsche finished well there they might have deprived Ferrari of the World Championship, but as in 1959, all four cars retired, two as a result of broken pistons.

An entirely new rear suspension design was a feature of the RS 61, using upper and lower triangular wishbones on each side, the lower ones located by longitudinal rods. The front axle trailing links had greater offset, and the upper bodywork was substantially revised for Le Mans, literally cutting off the rear fairing just ahead of the rear axles. It was a distinctive shape which further reduced drag on the long straight, higher power outputs making their contribution.

The RS 61 remained current until the 904 model was fully operational in 1964, though greater successes came with the installation of the 2 litre, flat-eight engine with 210 bhp. This was prepared for 1982 with two capacities, 1.5 litres (180 bhp) for Formula 1 and 2.0 litres for sports cars, later being taken out to 2.2 litres for a career which extended to 1968.

The four-cylinder engine seemed to be nearing the end of its development in 1961, and was not always as reliable as it should have been, though remarkably it was carried over to the 904 model in 1964 on the grounds that it was less specialized than the eight-cylinder, and the new 911-based six-cylinder was not fully developed.

No outright successes were claimed in 1961 and 1962, when Ferrari dominated. Each season consisted of only four events, sportscar racing being in one of its periodic declines. After two successive Targa Florio defeats, though, Porsche bounced back in 1963 with a fine victory for the type 718 W-RS eight-cylinder RS model driven by Jo Bonnier and Carlo Abate. Victory had seemed close in 1962 but the team was let down by its new disc brake system, and the Porsche-ATE development was certainly

*The high tail section was designed for Le Mans, but customer versions of the RS 60 had a more familiar engine cover. The tall windscreen was stipulated by the regulations of 1960.*

*The RS 61 model, which competed from 1961 to 1964, had its wheelbase extended from 210 to 220 cm (82 to 86 in), and the rear suspension was completely new with contemporary racing pattern upper and lower triangulated wishbones.*

in good working order for 1963. The Porsche RS enjoyed much more success in the European Hillclimb Championship, Edgar Barth taking the title in 1963 and in 1964 in a venerable 2 litre, 8-cylinder model, known affectionately as 'Grandma'.

While developing specialized RS models for World Championship racing, Porsche looked after its customers by producing high performance versions of the 356 models. The top models in the catalogues were given the 'Carrera' name, denoting that they were intended for competitions, and were sometimes handled by works drivers. The power unit chosen was the complex, Fuhrmann–designed 547 four-cylinder, originally at 1.5 litre capacity and 110 bhp, later with the 1.6 litre version and 115 bhp.

The 356A 1500 GS Carrera won countless awards for customers, and fared well in international events. In the Reims 12-Hour sports car race in 1957 356 Carreras took the top two places in the GT category, and at Sebring the following year — when developed with aluminium doors, front and rear hoods, and larger brakes — the 1600 GT class fell to Huschke von Hanstein and Herbert Linge. The Targa Florio was another happy hunting ground, von Hanstein and Baron Pucci finishing sixth overall in the 1958 event and third overall the following year.

The 356B 1600 GS Carrera GTL is a collector's item, based on the 1959 356B chassis. Special aluminium bodies were

*The Carrera Abarth at Le Mans, on its way to tenth place in the hands of Herbert Linge and Heini Walter.*

designed by Franco Scaglione and manufactured by Zagato in Turin, with assembly by Abarth. Twenty of these special models were made for the 1960 season, and were admired for their sleek lines as much as their sheer performance; the height was reduced by 5 in (13 cm), the bulbous looks were removed as 4.7 in were cut from the width, and some 100 kg (220 lb) was taken off the kerb weight, reducing it to 780 kg (1,716 lb).

Linge and Paul Strähle took a GTL to sixth place overall in the 1960 Targa Florio, winning their class, and Strähle followed up with a class win at the Nürburgring. Linge and Heini Walter drove the GTL to tenth place overall at Le Mans, and the following year class wins were recorded at Sebring, the Targa Florio, the Nürburgring and Le Mans.

The final form of the 356B 2000 GS/GT Carrera was seen in the 1963 season, the aluminium body being designed by Ferdinand 'Butzi' Porsche and built by the factory. Only two were made, and the cars were powered by the 2 litre, four-cylinder engine rated at 130 bhp. Barth and Linge finished fourth overall in the Targa Florio, and were fourth again at the Nürburgring, winning the class on both occasions.

*The 356B Carrera Abarth was a special series of 20 cars produced, in 1960, for customers. The Turin specialist Carlo Abarth designed and built the cars, which were lower than standard and weighed 140 kg less than a standard 356B. The 1,588 cc engine developed 115 bhp, with twin overhead camshafts and dual ignition.*

**Left and below** *A poor shot of the Elva-Porsche in action in the 1964 European Hillclimb Championship, and a better one of the same car in an American display. Edgar Barth and Herbert Müller drove the car, which was fitted with the 8-cylinder engine. Other Elvas in private hands were powered by four and six-cylinder engines.*

Many customers felt that, at 550 kg (1,210 lb), the type 718 was rather uncompetitive by 1963, and the Elva Mk VII became a popular mount for the four-cylinder 1.7 litre engine, which was developing a healthy 183 bhp. A number of Elva-Porsches were prepared for SCCA racing, and in 1964 Porsche took the unusual step of preparing one with the eight-cylinder engine, for the European Hillclimb Championship.

Although the Elva-Porsche was 30 kg (66 lb) lighter than the 718 Spyder it was not nearly as stiff. Edgar Barth won the opening round of the 1964 season, at Rossfeld, beating Herbert Müller in Barth's regular 718, but the German then decided to revert to the 718. With this car he won the EHCC for the second successive year, and Müller was runner-up in the Elva-Porsche.

# *Porsche type 718/2*

Porsche won two Formula 2 races without actually building an F2 car! At that time there was no rule that the wheels had to be exposed, and at the Nürburgring in 1957 Edgar Barth took pole position for the F2 race driving an RS Spyder, then won the race outright. In 1958 Bonnier won the F2 race supporting the French GP at Reims, and the Zuffenhausen engineers decided that is was time to prepare a special car, though basically it was a rebodied Spyder with the driver seated in the centre, instead of the left side.

The four-cylinder 1.5 litre engine developed 155 bhp initially, and up to 174 bhp in the 1961 season when Kugelfischer fuel injection was tried, without convincing the designers. The new type 718 six-speed transmission was another feature

*In 1962 the type 718 Coupé had its raised tail cover cut off, a new idea in aerodynamics. This one is driven by Dan Gurney on his way to tenth place at the Nürburgring, with Jo Bonnier. Under the hood is the new 2 litre, 8-cylinder engine which developed 210 bhp, compared with 180 bhp for the 1.5 litre F1 engine.*

**Above** *The 1962 version of the 718, the GTR Coupé, was visually similar to the RS 61 coupé and had only minor suspension changes. Using the 8-cylinder engine, Nino Vaccarella and Jo Bonnier drove this one to third place in the '62 Targa Florio.*

**Right** *The Formula 2, 4-cylinder Porsche qualified to be a Formula 1 car under new regulations in 1961, though outclassed with its 165 bhp engine. This is Jo Bonnier at Solitude.*

of the car, also used in the sports car programme.

The open-wheel version was preferred, though, and Stirling Moss was so impressed with one that he persuaded his entrant, Rob Walker, to buy it for the 1960 season. It took Moss five races to score his first victory, at Aintree, where he was followed across the line by the Porsches of Jo Bonnier and Graham Hill. Moss won again at Zeltweg, the Austrian airfield track, while Bonnier won the F2 race supporting the German Grand Prix. A number of other high placings were taken by Herrmann, Barth, Hill, Bonnier and Gurney, enabling Porsche to win the F2 Constructors' Championship against stiff competition from Cooper and Lotus.

Formula 1 regulations were changed for 1961, reducing the maximum capacity to 1.5 litres, and Porsche automatically had a Grand Prix contender ready for action. Dan Gurney finished fifth overall in the Monaco Grand Prix, earning the make's first ever World Championship points in single-seaters; and he did even better at Reims, where he was second to Giancarlo Baghetti's Ferrari, at Monza where he was second to Phil Hill's Ferrari, and at Watkins Glen where he was second again, this time to Innes Ireland's Lotus. The Reims race was a real cliff-hanger, Gurney finishing just 0.1 sec behind the Ferrari in a slipstreaming finish, and in the course of the season he earned 21 points to finish third equal in the F1 driver's championship. Phil Hill won the title, and von Trips was the posthumous runner-up after losing his life at Monza. The Ferrari and Porsche teams mourned him alike, but in terms of results it was Ferrari's year ... though Porsche had done particularly well, no question.

Encouraged by these successes Porsche prepared the type 804 Formula 1 car for the 1962 season, using the flat 8-cylinder engine. The tubular spaceframe chassis resembled that of the 718, and had torsion bar springing front and rear, with upper and lower wishbones. The body was made of aluminium, and 'Butzi' Porsche had a hand in the styling.

The engine, type 753, had a bore and stroke of 66 x 54.6 mm for a capacity of 1,494 cc, and two camshafts on each bank driven by shafts and bevel gears. A horizontal axial fan made of plastic cooled the eight Chromal cylinders, and four Weber 38 mm carburettors adjusted the fuel mixture.

Porsche were a little disappointed to see only 180 bhp, believing that Ferrari had 190 bhp or more, but Gurney was competitive from the start. The 804 was ready for its debut in the Dutch Grand Prix at Zandvoort, the first round of the championship in May, but after making a good start the American went off the road, though he was able to recover and finish, albeit well down the order. The Dutch count, de Beaufort, saved the day by finishing sixth overall in his F2 specification Porsche.

**Below and right** *Porsche's first and only car designed for Grand Prix racing was the type 804. It was powered by the 1.5 litre, flat-eight engine developing 180 bhp. Dan Gurney is pictured at the Nouveau Monde hairpin at Rouen, on his way to victory in the 1962 French Grand Prix. The line drawing shows the spaceframe chassis layout and suspension details.*

The next appearance for the 804 was at Rouen, the French Grand Prix in July, and Gurney was backed by a second car for Bonnier. The American was sixth quickest in practice, ran in third place behind Jim Clark (Lotus) and Graham Hill (BRM), and took the lead when they retired. He held on to it easily, beating Tony Maggs' Cooper-Climax by a full lap ... and that was Porsche's first, and only Formula 1 World Championship victory.

There were great expectations for the German Grand Prix, attended by a quarter of a million spectators in wet and foggy weather, and they certainly had a race to remember, though the result was not what they hoped for: Graham Hill won the race in his BRM with John Surtees 2.5 sec behind in his Lola-Climax, and Gurney 2.9 sec behind him. Bonnier was sixth at Monza, Gurney fifth at Watkins Glen, so the season ended on a down note.

Porsche then withdrew from single-seater racing, to concentrate on sports car events which it knew better, and from which it probably reaped more benefit. The flat-eight, in 2 litre form, gave great service during the 1960s as we shall see.

The Porsche company was undergoing a major transition in 1963 and, as happened ten years later, product engineering was to play a major part in racing car design. The company had withdrawn from Formula 1 racing but still had the twin-cam Carrera engine, designed by Dr Ernst Fuhrmann, available in 1.5 and 2.0 litre form, to power the top versions of a new racing car.

Notably though there was the new 6-cylinder, 2-litre engine available from the 901 road car, announced in September 1963 and put into production as the 911, in September 1964. Rapid development of more powerful versions, for racing and rallying, would continue to be part of Porsche's philosophy, and what better way to do this than to homologate the 6-cylinder in a new racing car?

Ing Hans Tomala, who developed the power unit for the 911, became the 'father' of the new racing car intended for the Grand Touring Sports category, and 904 happened to be its drawing board number. Unlike all of Porsche's previous racing car designs, Tomala decided to give the 904 a sheet-steel platform chassis which would be stiffened by the rollover bar, and especially by the glass-fibre bodywork which was bonded to the chassis.

**Below and right** *Two views of the Porsche 904, produced in series in 1964. A minimum of 100 needed to be made for homologation into the GT Sport category, nearly all with the 4-cylinder type 547 engine producing up to 185 bhp.*

The design was well advanced when the decision was made to equip the 904 with the 4-cylinder Carrera engine from production, rather than the new 6-cylinder. Both were able to deliver around 180 bhp, an excellent figure for a carburated, production-based 2 litre, but it was felt that the 'six' was just too new and not sufficiently developed to be released to 100 private customers around the world, especially as many of them had plenty of experience of the 'four'. Management made a pragmatic decision to build and sell, and homologate 100 examples with the 4-cylinder, and to make a further 100 examples for the 1965 season with the 6-cylinder. As it turned out though, a second series was never made. Instead, the first run reached 120 examples of which 104 had 4-cylinder engines and of the remainder, retained by the factory, ten had 6-cylinder engines and six had 8-cylinder engines.

The price quoted for the 904 Carrera GTS was very attractive at DM 27,900 (about £2,800 at the prevailing rate of exchange), and the model offered 155 bhp with a road-legal exhaust system or 180 bhp with a racing exhaust. Wheels were pressed steel, 5J x 15, which hardly seemed adequate even by standards of the day though sufficient for a car which weighed about 650 kg (1,430 lb) at the kerb (the type 550 had weighed about 500 kg

(1,100 lb) at equivalent specification). In some circumstances the 550 might have been quicker, certainly uphill, but the 904 was as rugged as any production car and ideal for customer use in endurance events, one of its main attributes being easy maintenance.

The bodywork, as stated, was glass-fibre rather than aluminium, and approximately doubled the 904's torsional stiffness. The coupé design looked right, from the start, although it was not wind tunnel tested. The headlamps were set far back, almost at the leading edge of the front tyres and shielded by conical Perspex covers, and the only 'spoiling' of the shape was caused by air ducts behind the doors feeding the rear brakes, which overheated badly in tests.

Development of the 904 was completed in six months, testing being confined to the new skid pan at Weissach and to the Nürburgring race circuit, and two cars ran at Sebring in March 1964 in the prototype class, since the series of 100 cars had not yet passed inspection. Edgar Barth and Herbert Linge experienced clutch problems and finished twentieth, but Briggs Cunningham and Lake Underwood enjoyed a clear run and finished in ninth place overall, winning the 2 litre category.

A month later, and duly homologated, Porsche 904s caused a major upset by finishing first and second overall in the Targa Florio, Colin Davis and Antonio Pucci leading Herbert Linge and Gianni Balzarini. Porsche's two type 550 Spyders had both broken and the 4.7 litre Shelby Cobras proved to have much more power than handling. The 904s, on the other hand, were nimble, easy to drive on the bumpy, mountainous roads and, above all, totally reliable. The last factor was to be seen time and again in the next two seasons, for at Spa seven finished out of eight, all five finished the Le Mans 24-hours — that of Robert Buchet and Guy Ligier finishing seventh overall — and at Reims all eight finished safely.

There was nothing to touch the Porsche 904 in GT racing, and its durability was appreciated by customers in road events too: in the 6,000 kilometre Tour de France 904s were placed third to sixth overall, behind a pair of Ferrari GTOs, and in January 1965 Eugen Bohringer and Rolf Wütherich finished second overall in the Monte Carlo Rally, an event so snowy that the mid-engined car's chances of finishing, let alone doing well, were almost nil! In that same event Herbert Linge and Peter Falk, both factory employees, gave the 911 model its competitions debut and finished in fifth place overall, and second to the 904 in the GT class. That was the start of a new era in Porsche's competitions history, as they might have guessed.

Porsche's job was done, so far as the GT models were concerned, once the 100 cars had been sold but not until the 911 was in production did further development take place, installing both the 6-cylinder and 8-cylinder engines for factory entries in the prototype category. Late in 1964 Barth and Davis took a 235 bhp, 8-cylinder 904 to third place in the Paris 1,000 Kms at Montlhèry, behind a pair of 3.3 litre Ferraris.

By now Ing Tomala had left the company, replaced by Dr Ferry Porsche's nephew Ferdinand Piëch, and the pace of development quickened. Piëch had little use for the 904, with its heavy and simplistic design, and was personally in favour of extreme weight-saving by every possible means. The customers could have their 904 GTS models uprated to 185 bhp with larger inlet valves and new camshafts, all they needed to continue to dominate the GT category, and the 6-cylinder and 8-cylinder

*They called it the 'Kangaroo', which might have been Gerhard Mitter's description of its handling. The 904 Bergspyder developed for the 1965 European Hillclimb Championship, powered by the eight-cylinder engine, was torsionally weak, and heavy modifications were needed to make it competitive.*

versions were raced by the factory purely as a stopgap until the 906 model could be readied for the 1966 season.

The variety of Porsche 904 configurations was easily noted at the Targa Florio, held in Sicily in May, where four 2 litre models finished behind the winning Ferrari. One of them, driven by Colin Davis and Gerhard Mitter, was an unique spyder (open) version powered by the 235 bhp eight-cylinder engine. It was rejected by Jo Bonnier as being insufficiently stiff in torsion, which was probably the case, but Davis and Mitter finished well in second place. Third was the 210 bhp, 6-cylinder 904/6 of Herbert Linge and Umberto Maglioli, and fourth the 8-cylinder 904 coupé of Bonnier and Graham Hill. Fifth were Günther Klass and Antonio Pucci in a 4-cylinder 904/GTS, winners of the GT category.

The 904's durability proved itself again at Le Mans, where Herbert Linge and Peter Nocker took fourth place overall in a 6-cylinder version, behind three 3.3 litre Ferraris, while in fifth place was a 4-cylinder 904. The 911 engine was constructed in magnesium alloy rather than aluminium, to save weight, and in 1969 this construction was transferred to the production line, improving the handling of the rear-engined road car.

The 911 engine was proved beyond doubt at Le Mans, where it covered 2,800 trouble free miles (4,505 km) at an average of 118 mph (190 km/h). The winning Ferrari 275LM completed 2,906 miles (4,676 km), and 13 laps was not much to give away in 24 hours to Maranello designs with an extra 100 horsepower.

The 8-cylinder engine, type 771, was raced only rarely, and then only in shorter events as it was not thought to be sufficiently reliable. That aspect was being worked on, and the engine would become increasingly effective in later designs of the 1960s.

Within the factory, the 6-cylinder 904s were referred to as 906s (the chassis plates also defined them as 906s) and this has always caused confusion about the succeeding model, the 906 Carrera 6. Retrospectively, the 6-cylinder 904s are called 904/6 models. Piëch had decided from the start to revert to spaceframe steel-tube construction, although the design was new and unlike that of the 718.

The first spaceframe chassis was given a run at the Ollon-Villars hillclimb in 1965, and following this exercise, and torsional tests, the frame was reinforced with additional tubes at the rear. The 906 would rely heavily on its chassis strength, since the detachable glass-fibre panels contributed very little to torsional stiffness.

This was the first Porsche to be tested in a wind tunnel, producing a drag figure of 0.36, while a more aerodynamic, 'longtail' bodystyle developed for Daytona and Le Mans produced a better figure of 0.326, and was up to 16 mph (25 km/h) faster in terminal speed.

All the running gear was transferred from the 904 including the 911's 6-cylinder engine, rated at 210 bhp with double Weber triple-choke carburettors, the 911's 5-speed transmission, brakes, suspensions and wheels. All the suspension joints were metallic, though, rather than with rubber blocks, since there were no plans to offer the 906 for road use. Another vital difference was the wheels which, although steel (in standard form) and 15 in (38 cm) in diameter, had much greater offset and were 7 in (18 cm) wide at the front and 9 in (23 cm) wide at the rear, improving the handling and braking characteristics.

The 906 proved to be no lighter than the 904, but its weight distribution was greatly enhanced by carrying the fuel in twin pannier tanks rather than under the front lid, the handling quality being maintained when the tanks were light. The front of the

*The 906, for the 1966 season, had a tubular spaceframe chassis, and was powered by the 2 litre 6-cylinder engine. Fifty were built for homologation, and those raced by the factory generally had 8-cylinder engines. Illustrated, the Udo Schutz/Günther Klass entry at the Nürburgring.*

*The longtail 906 bodywork was specially produced for Le Mans, reducing the drag figure to 0.326. Moving tail flaps, operated by the suspension, were in their infancy.*

car could therefore be lower, and a distinguishing feature of the 906 was its long, sloping rear window, coloured yellow, with rows of ventilating slats cut into the sides. Another feature, inspired perhaps by Mercedes in the 1950s, was the use of gull-wing doors, hinged at the top.

Only 50 cars had to be made now to qualify for the GT category but the production run eventually reached 65, of which 52 (sold) had the 210 bhp 6-cylinder engine, nine prototypes had Bosch fuel injection raising the power to 220 bhp, and four had the 4-cam, 8-cylinder engine now increased to 2.2 litre capacity and producing 260 bhp, also with Bosch fuel injection.

The longtail version was the first to appear, in the 1966 Daytona 24-Hours where Hans Herrmann/Herbert Linge had a trouble-free run to sixth place behind 7 litre Fords and 4.4 litre Ferraris. A month later a 'kurz' tail works car driven by Herrmann, Gerhard Mitter and Joe Buzzetta finished fourth behind a trio of 7 litre Fords.

Three different types of 906 formed the spearhead of the Targa Florio entry, one as homologated with carburettors for Pucci/Arena — and Scuderia Filipinetti had another, for Willy Mairesse/Herbert Müller — two with injection for Mitter/Bonnier and Herrmann/Dieter Glemser, and an 8-cylinder model for Colin Davis/Gunther Klass. A needle match was expected against a pair of 4 litre Ferraris, Klass being quickest in practice, but the race was mainly wet and Mitter went off the road, while Klass retired with broken suspension. The Ferraris wilted too, and Porsche's sixth victory in Sicily was earned by the Filipinetti car, rather to the factory's embarrassment.

Porsche's factory cars did not do well at the Nürburgring either, as the winged Chaparral and the works Ferraris duelled for victory. Jochen Rindt burned out his clutch at the start, Glemser went off the road and Klass's car broke a driveshaft. A 906 driven by Paul Hawkins and Bob Bondurant was placed fourth, and one result of this sortie was the decision to run only brand-new cars in important races ... one which would raise the cost of racing considerably, and keep the racing department at full stretch for the next four years!

Le Mans was, as usual, the highlight of the season, and there the 7 litre Fords were invincible. They took the top three places, as was only to be expected assuming reasonable reliability, while fuel injected, 6-cylinder 906 models took fourth, fifth and sixth places, Jo Siffert and Colin Davis leading the way. Seventh was a carburated 906 driven by Klass and Rolf Stommelen, winning the GT class.

*Fourth event for the 906 was the Targa Florio in 1966, where Willy Mairesse and Herbert Müller achieved a fine victory. The 6-cylinder engine was installed for this event.*

Throughout the 1966 and 1967 seasons the 906 was the regular GT class winner, while the factory moved on to its successor.

**Right** *Three of the five Porsche 906s entered for Le Mans in 1966. Although heavily outgunned by the 7 litre Fords, Porsches took fourth to seventh positions.*

**Below** *Jo Siffert and the British driver, Colin Davis, were fourth at Le Mans in 1966 with the 906 model. The six-cylinder engine developed 220 bhp with Bosch injection, while in seventh place Klass/Stommelen won the GT class with a carburated six-cylinder engine.*

*The 910 was the successor to the 906, though a more specialized design for factory use, and adaptable for six or eight cylinder engines. Behind the car, from left to right, Dr Ferry Porsche, Hans Mezger, Helmuth Bott, Richard Hetmann, Wolfgang Eyb, Ferdinand Piëch, Paul Hensler, Herr Schröder, Helmuth Flegl and Peter Falk.*

During the 1960s the European Mountain Championship continued to be a prestigious series for which Porsche, Ferrari and Abarth prepared special cars. These would usually be much lighter than the circuit models, and often included new features which would be tested and transferred to the racing programme if found to be suitable. Edgar Barth was the master of the mountains until 1964, but was destined to die of an illness, Lodovico Scarfiotti claimed the title for Ferrari in 1965, and in 1966 Gerhard Mitter won the crown back for Porsche in a lightweight version of the 906, despite having his foot in plaster after an accident at Spa. For the last event of the 1966 series, at Schauinsland, Mitter drove the 910 for the first time.

The type numbers go out of sequence at this point, the 910 preceding the 907, 908, 909 and 917 models in that order, although particularly as regards their chassis there was always a close connection. The 910 was being prepared for the factory team's main effort in 1967, and like preceding models it would accept the 6- or 8-cylinder engines.

In concept the 910 was similar to the 906, although the front track was increased, and 13 in (33 cm) diameter magnesium alloy wheels were used, with 8 in (21 cm) rim widths at the front and 9.5 in (24 cm) at the rear. Weight-saving was the order of the day, though, and the 910 was some 65 kg (143 lb) lighter than the 906, at 590 kg (1,298 lb), through having lighter bodywork and wheels, beryllium brake discs, titanium hubs, and oil was taken to the front cooler and back through the chassis tubes.

The bodywork was further refined in the wind tunnel and the

*The Porsche 910 model was raced by the factory for one season, in 1967, taking the top three places in the Targa Florio and the top four at the Nürburgring. Most were powered by six-cylinder engines—this photograph is of Vic Elford at the start of the Targa Florio, in which he finished third with the 910/6—but the event was won by Rolf Stommelen/Paul Hawkins in an 8-cylinder version.*

rear window glass set vertical, while the doors were front-hinged for greater safety at high speed (the 'langheck' version, however, still had elongated plastic covering the engine bay). Altogether 28 910s were made, all initially for the factory team, but in 1968 the requirement for homologation was reduced to 25 examples only so the model was duly homologated and 25 were sold, many of them having raced only once.

Siffert and Herrmann gave the 910 a customary solid debut outing in the Daytona 24-Hours, finishing fourth behind three 4-litre Ferraris, while at Sebring the works Porsches were third and fourth, behind 7-litre Fords, and at Monza they were third and fifth, again behind Ferraris. At Spa the results had a new look as Jacky Ickx and Alan Rees, in a 5.7 litre Mirage-bodied Ford GT40, took a magnificent victory in wet conditions, followed by Siffert and Herrmann in a 910.

No fewer than six 910s were entered by Porsche for the Targa Florio, three with 6-cylinder engines and three with 2.2 litre flat-eights. The principal opposition came from Nino Vac-

carella/Lodovico Scarfiotti in a Ferrari P4 but, after leading the first lap Vaccarella crashed at Cerda on the second. The strongest Ferraris, and de Adamich's 2-litre Alfa Romeo 33, fell out and Porsches made a clean sweep of the results, Paul Hawkins/Rolf Stommelen winning in a 2.2 litre model followed by Cella/Biscaldi and Vic Elford/Jochen Neerpasch in 6-cylinder versions.

Six 910s were entered again at the Nürburgring, a 'home' event for Porsche but one in which the Stuttgart firm had never been an outright winner. The 1967 race made up for that, and in the absence of Ferrari opposition Porsche claimed the top four places, though the 7 litre Chaparral had gone ahead until stopped by transmission failure. The 2.2 litre 910s, in fact, proved unreliable as Stommelen and Siffert dropped out with broken valves, perhaps due to over-revving, and the first three places were taken by the 6-cylinder models driven by Udo Schutz/Joe Buzzetta, Gerhard Koch/Paul Hawkins, and Vic Elford/Jochen Neerpasch.

*The 'Berg' version of the 910, powered by the 2 litre flat eight engine developing 270 bhp. In its final form the weight was pared down to 400 kg (880 lb), and Gerhard Mitter won his third European Hillclimb Championship title with this car in 1968.*

A new version, the 907, appeared at Le Mans and finished in fifth place, while sixth was the 6-cylinder 910 of Jo Siffert and Hans Herrmann. By the end of the season Porsche stood a chance of winning the World Sports Car Championship, since Chaparral, Ford and Ferrari had split the scoring overall, but to do so they would have to finish ahead of the Ferraris at Brands Hatch, in the BOAC 500.

The 2.2 litre, 8-cylinder Porsche 910s would need all the luck in the world, as the high-winged Chaparral driven by Phil Hill and Mike Spence sped to victory. Chris Amon and Jackie Stewart were Ferrari's pace-setters, Jo Siffert and Bruce McLaren were Porsche's, and at the end of a tense battle the Ferrari was second, just one lap ahead of Siffert and McLaren.

After many years of being 2 litre class winners, the Porsches were now looking more and more like outright winners, and the FIA's decision to introduce new rules in 1968 would be entirely to Porsche's advantage, as the 7-litre Ford and Chaparral contenders would be swept away. To fill the gap, Porsche had the 907 model fully developed.

The 910 race programme was ended at the close of the 1967 season, but an ultra-light version was prepared for Gerhard Mitter to campaign in the mountains in 1968, and he duly won his third consecutive title. In spyder form, and despite its rather heavier 8-cylinder engine, the 910 Bergspyder was reduced in weight, incredibly, to 410 kg (902 lb) with almost translucent bodywork, titanium springs, hubs and other components, an aluminium spaceframe chassis, and by deleting the alternator. Even the saving of a few grammes, for instance in the switch-gear, was considered useful.

Mitter became the European champion for the third time in his special 910 by winning the Group 7 class in every event, his closest competitor being Dieter Quester in the BMW. Scarfiotti, though, was killed in an accident at Rossfeld, having switched from Ferrari to a Porsche 910, and it is fair to say that this was the final season in which the Mountain Championship would carry much prestige. Ferrari had already withdrawn, and Porsche would do so after preparing one more contender.

Porsche had been experimenting heavily with aerodynamic aids, though not with the high aerofoils which suited the powerful Chaparral, and in 1968 Mitter's 910 Bergspyder featured moving flaps at the rear, actuated by spring movement. As the spring was decompressed, in a corner or over a brow, the flap would be raised and apply downforce, and the system was soon transferred to the race cars which would enjoy greater benefit at higher speeds.

The 907 model had a shorter competitions life than any other Porsche, less than a year, but it was a successful model. Basically it was much like the 910 but with right-hand steering — most tracks run to the right, and the driver's weight is then better placed in the right-hand seat — and was narrower above the waist, so that the 'langheck' version would be faster still at Le Mans, or around the Daytona banking. The drag coefficient was reduced from 0.3 to 0.273, an extremely low figure for a racing car with some aerodynamic downforce, and further modifications included revised front suspension, with shorter, lighter springs and more progressive damping, and ventilated disc brakes were standard equipment.

For its debut at Le Mans the 907 was powered by the 6-cylinder engine, still developing 220 bhp, and Siffert and Herrmann had a trouble-free drive to fifth place overall, behind two 7 litre Fords and two 4 litre Ferraris. They averaged 125 mph (200 km/h) for the entire 24 hours and finished seven laps ahead of Stommelen and Neerpasch in the 910, also with a 6-cylinder engine.

Only one race remained in the 1967 season, at Brands Hatch, and there the tables were turned as the Siffert/McLaren finished

*Porsche's 907 model was much like the 910 but had right-hand steering, a belated recognition of the advantages on right-hand circuits. To reduce drag a narrow windscreen was featured on the Le Mans 907/6 entry which Siffert and Herrmann drove to fifth place overall.*

in third place, ahead of the 8-cylinder 907 driven by Herrmann and Neerpasch. The 907s were campaigned by the factory in the first half of the 1968 season, until the 908 model was developed to winning form, always with the 2.2 litre 8-cylinder engine which now gave 270 bhp with reliability. Also in 1968 a new 6-speed gearbox was introduced, intended primarily for the 908.

The new Appendix J regulations for 1968 placed a limit of 3 litres on 'prototypes' which must weigh at least 650 kg (1,430 lb) (though the minimum weight was abolished after one year) and 5 litres on homologated sports cars, such as the Ford GT40 and Lola T70, so the 2.2 litre 907s were theoretically at a disadvantage.

Rival teams were preparing new or updated cars though, and with reliability on their side the Porsches were never outclassed. The main opposition at the opening rounds, at Daytona and Sebring, came from the Gulf–sponsored J.W. Automotive Ford

*A remarkable victory in the Targa Florio was achieved by Vic Elford and Umberto Maglioli in 1968, their 907/8 having been delayed 16 minutes by a burst tyre. Elford was the hero of the day.*

GT40s, with Jacky Ickx leading the team, but although faster where speed mattered, especially on the banking, the Fords did not enjoy total reliability. The 1968 season opened with two overwhelming victories for the factory Porsche 907s, which claimed the top three places at Daytona ahead of a Ford Mustang! Vic Elford and Jochen Neerpasch won the race but their car was also shared by Jo Siffert and Hans Herrmann, whose second-placed car was delayed by throttle linkage trouble, and by Rolf Strommelen whose car was crashed by Gerhard Mitter. The history books do not show many race winners with five drivers!

ing only one lap fewer than the previous year's 7 litre Ford, and Elford and Neerpasch finished second after having a front upright changed. Wheel bearings continued to be a major problem throughout the season, costing Porsche a couple of victories, and proved to be due to the lower heat transfer properties of the titanium hubs, cured by improving the grease.

*Rico Steinemann and Dieter Spoerry drove this 907/8 to second place at Le Mans in 1968, Porsche's highest-ever placing in the 24-hour race. Already that season the 907/8 had taken the top three places in the Daytona 24-Hours, finished first and second at Sebring, and won the Targa Florio.*

Siffert and Herrmann seemed almost certain to win the BOAC 500 at Brands Hatch until a wheel bearing failure stopped their 907, and a narrow victory was gained by Ickx and Brian Redman in the Gulf-Ford GT40, a mere 22 sec ahead of Mitter and Scarfiotti in a 907, with Elford and Neerpasch third. The day was marred for everyone by news of Jim Clark's fatal accident at the Hockenheimring, in a Formula 2 Lotus, and a month later Scarfiotti was killed in a freak hillclimb accident.

Porsche's effort was split at Monza where two new 908 coupés were entered for Siffert/Herrmann and Mitter/Scarfiotti, plus a 907 for Stommelen and Neerpasch. The 908s proved unreliable, and the 907 was beaten into second place by the GT40 driven by Paul Hawkins/David Hobbs.

Four factory 907s were entered for the Targa Florio, all 8-cylinder versions as usual, but all ran into various difficulties and for some time a rare victory by Alfa Romeo was likely. Vic Elford's 907, shared with Umberto Maglioli, was delayed a full 16 minutes by a loose front wheel which led to a tyre failure. After finishing a long lap on his space-saver wheel Elford continued the race, hopelessly out of contention, but drove an inspired race to pass the Alfas and record one of Porsche's most spectacular victories, eight minutes quicker than the previous year's winning 910! That was the 907's last World Championship success since Porsche's major effort switched to the 908 model, but Gerhard Mitter and Jo Schlesser finished second at Spa, and a 907/8 was then lent to Rico Steinemann and Dieter Spörry for Le Mans. Doubts about the 8-cylinder engine's suitability for 24-hour races were dispelled as the private team finished second, behind the Gulf Ford of Pedro Rodriguez and Lucien Bianchi ... and pushed the works 908 of Stommelen and Neerpasch down to third.

Both the 908 and 909 appeared during the 1968 season, the 908 circuit car a few months before the 909 'berg' machine, but the 909 is significant only in being a forerunner of the 908/3 development; as such, it has priority.

The 910 'berg' model earned Gerhard Mitter his third successive mountain title, and when that was assured he was offered the type 909 to finish the season. After testing it at Gaisberg, though, Mitter decided that he preferred his 910 so it was driven there, and in the final round at Mont Ventoux, by Rolf Stommelen.

The 909 differed mainly in having the gearbox and differential transposed, the gearbox behind the engine and the differential at the back, a system tried later by March for their Formula 1 car in the interests of reducing the polar moment of inertia.

*Porsche's last hillclimb car was the 909, which appeared only twice in 1969. It was a forerunner of the 908/03 circuit car in having its 5-speed gearbox turned round, positioned in front of the differential.*

The wheelbase was not lengthened at all, as would have been expected, since the driver was moved further forward in the chassis, his feet ahead of the front wheel axis, and the front wheels were moved back by 3.6 cm (1.4 in). The weight distribution was moved forward as a consequence and this should have improved the handling, Stommelen believing that it did but Mitter disagreeing.

Like the 907, the 909 had right-hand steering, the 2 litre 8-cylinder engine, and wider wheels. An interesting feature was the nitrogen-filled titanium sphere which contained 20 litres (4.4 gallons) of fuel, delivered to the engine under high pressure. Even so, the 909 was 20 kg (44 lb) heavier than the 910 Berg, at 430 kg (946 lb).

The engine ran badly for Stommelen at Gaisberg, perhaps due to the pressure at which the fuel was delivered (215 psi), and at Mont Ventoux a normal fuel pump was installed. The car then ran perfectly, Stommelen finishing 5.5 sec behind Mitter who established a new record.

The 909 thus had the shortest competition record of any Porsche, and no wins, but was an important part of the 908's development.

At the outset the 908 model, seen for the first time at the Le Mans trials in April 1968, was almost identical, visually, to the 907. The coupé body form was rarely used though, the 908 more familiarly having an open cockpit style, and in 1969 the more aerodynamic 'Sole' bodywork became the standard for the 908/02 version.

The main development was the 3 litre engine, an entirely new flat-eight which replaced the complex 'Fuhrmann' engine, designed at the start of the decade as a Formula 1 unit. With a maximum displacement of 2.2 litres the previous engine had a maximum power output of 270-275 bhp, while to take advantage of the new 3 litre/5 litre rules the 908's engine had an output of 320 bhp straight away, and a minimum of 350 bhp in the 1969 season.

Dipl Ing Hans Mezger was responsible for the power unit which was based as much as possible on the 911 6-cylinder, including the 84 x 66 mm bore/stroke dimensions, the addition of two cylinders raising the capacity by 33 per cent to 2,921 cc. It had dry sump lubrication of course, as did the special 6-speed gearbox used latterly on the 910 and 907 models for development purposes, but since it weighed a massive 25 kg (55 lb) more

*The 908 model appeared first in coupé form at Monza, and again at Le Mans where Rolf Stommelen/Jochen Neerpasch claimed third place overall, behind the Ford GT40 and the Steinemann/Spoerry 907/8. The 908's 3 litre 8-cylinder engine was entirely new, though based on the production six, and developed 320–360 bhp.*

than the previous 5-speed transmission, a new 5-speed was developed as quickly as possible.

Mezger — who takes credit for all subsequent power units up to and including the TAG Formula 1 V6 — retained the air-cooling layout though with a vertical fan driven, originally, by a cogged belt, later by twin vee belts, which also drove the alternator, though neither was to prove very satisfactory. As usual there were two valves per cylinder and twin-plug ignition was used, although rival 3 litre designs from Ford-Cosworth (DFV V8) and Ferrari 312P (V12) both had four valves per cylinder and developed at least 420 bhp. Porsche usually had a major weight advantage, close to the 650 kg (1,430 lb) minimum in 1968, good aerodynamics, and was rarely troubled by a 70 bhp handicap. In 1971 a four-valve layout was tested with water cooling for the heads, and although it was not adopted the design was developed for the 1978 season.

In order to simplify the exhaust system the flat-8 had a two-plane crankshaft, unlike the type 771 2.2 litre which had a flat-plane crankshaft. It meant that the secondary forces were not balanced but it was not anticipated that consequent vibration would be important. As in the 911, the twin overhead camshafts on each bank were driven by chains rather than gears, calling for tensioners.

With only minor developments the chassis, brakes, steering and even the coupé bodywork were from the 907, including the right-hand steering which was now established. The 908 engine was slightly longer than the type 771, having larger bores, and was 18 kg (40 lb) heavier at 178 kg (392.6 lb), but it had a far better power:weight ratio and the new car should have been quicker straight away.

The early outings were extremely disappointing, even embarrassing, by Porsche's standards. At the Le Mans trials there were several failures of the fan's cogged belt drive, which was made more reliable straight away by substituting twin vee belts: the gear linkage was troublesome, and a driveshaft broke. Worse, the 908s were slower than the 907s had been a year before, all the cars tested (including the 907s) proving unstable on wider wheels.

The 908's race debut at Monza was a technical disaster with two broken driveshafts, a broken clutch cable and gearbox thrust washers being the tally for practice, and further difficulties in the race included a broken driveshaft 'doughnut' on the Siffert/Herrmann car and three separate breakages of the clutch cable on that of Mitter and Scarfiotti. The drivers reported the engine as being rough and noisy, with severe vibration going through the car at over 7,000 rpm. As a result the alternators and starter motors were breaking regularly.

Luckily the 907 had already scored a lot of points for the works team, first at Daytona and Sebring, second at Brands Hatch and Monza, and the 907 was used once more at the Targa Florio, enabling Vic Elford and Umberto Maglioli to record a spectacular victory.

The first success for the 908 came at the Nürburgring in May, Jo Siffert and Vic Elford winning after a race-long, six-and-a-half-hour battle with the Gulf GT40 of Jacky Ickx and Paul Hawkins. Flurries of snow fell, the track was never completely dry, and Siffert spun twice in the heat of the battle. Ickx was superb that day, Hawkins a little disappointing, and the GT40 finished close up in third place behind the second 908 driven by Herrmann and Stommelen. Many of the 908's problems had been cured, though not the worrying engine vibrations, and they now ran on 15 in (38.5 cm) diameter wheels which allowed larger brake discs to be fitted (also, Formula 1 teams had now moved on to the larger wheels, for which better tyres were available from Dunlop). A week later at Spa, it poured with rain and Ickx was in his element, Brian Redman proving himself an ideal co-driver. They finished a lap ahead of Mitter and Jo Schlesser in a 907 (Porsche continued to split its effort, still unsure of the new model), while Siffert and Herrmann were third in the 908. Engine vibration had been reduced, but not cured, by changing the firing order and fitting extra counterweights.

The suspension-operated moving tail flaps were on the cars for Watkins Glen, and became a standard feature having been tested on the 'berg' 910, and one of the 908s had an aluminium, rather than steel spaceframe chassis, saving 20 kg (44 lb). Since the engineers were concerned about its strength the entire chassis was pressurized and an air valve fitted at the rear so that, like a tyre, the chassis could be checked for pressure regularly. Any cracks or breakages, of course, would be detected immediately, rather than during stripdown after the race.

Although larger wheel bearings had been fitted, following early-season failures, two of the four 908s retired from the American race with bearing failure, later proved conclusively to be due to an inadequate specification for the grease. George Follmer's 908 went out with its engine over-revved, and Siffert/Herrmann/Tetsu Ikuzawa had a chapter of problems while limping to the finish, out of the top 10.

The half-points Zeltweg 500 Kms was not, perhaps, long enough to show the 908's continuing weaknesses but after winning the race, and completing the slowing-down lap, Jo Siffert

*Four longtail 908s were entered for Le Mans in 1968, but all suffered alternator problems due to engine vibration. Only one reached the finish, in third place.*

admitted that there was no drive to the rear wheels, later diagnosed as a broken output shaft from the engine to the gearbox.

The Le Mans 24-Hour race was postponed from June to September in 1968 due to industrial strife, but that turned out not to be Porsche's salvation. Any inherent weaknesses would be bound to show up, and sure enough all four longtail 908s were stopped repeatedly by vibration-induced alternator failures. Siffert and Herrmann retired with a broken gearbox casing, in fact, two more were forced into retirement, while Stommelen and Neerpasch managed to coax their 908 to the finish, in third place despite spending nearly an hour and a half in the pits. By winning easily in their Gulf GT40, Pedro Rodriguez and Lucien Bianchi enabled the J.W. Automotive Ford team to claim the World Championship, while Dieter Spörry and Rico Steinemann finished second in their works-loaned 907.

The CSI's decision to abolish the 650 kg (1,430 lb) minimum weight limit enabled Porsche to reduce the 908's weight dramatically, firstly by producing the Spyder open-deck bodywork and removing the large and heavy windscreen. The ruling body's other major decision, to reduce the homologation number for sports cars from 50 to 25, also inspired Porsche's decision to produce the 917, but no one outside the factory knew anything about that until March 1969!

A host of major and minor developments transformed the 908 for the 1969 season. The weight was immediately reduced from 660 kg (1,452 lb) to just 600 kg (1,320 lb), the new type 916 5-speed transmission making an important contribution, and the engine, now with an 85 mm bore (capacity 2,997 cc) had a flat-plane crank which removed all the unwanted vibration, only at the expense of a more complicated exhaust system. Extended testing at Monza in January 1969, prior to the Daytona 24-Hours, was halted as both cars crashed and burned out, one perhaps due to steering failure, the other to ice forming on the track.

The significance of that became clear when all five cars entered for the American endurance race retired for the self-same reason — the breakage of an aluminium gear driving the intermediate shaft of the camshaft drive. The 908s were certainly quick enough and when the last Porsche retired it was 45 laps ahead of the Lola T70 (Mark Donohue/Chuck Parsons) which eventually won the race.

Lack of adequate testing could be blamed, too, for a crop of chassis breakages at Sebring, a tube holding the rear suspension in place fracturing on all five cars. Three of them reached the finish after rebuilds, Stommelen and Buzzetta in third place.

So far the Porsche 908 had not been an outstanding success, but at Brands Hatch and thereafter it proved almost completely reliable and well able to deal with increasing opposition from the new Ferrari 312P, usually a solo entry for Pedro Rodriguez and Chris Amon. The new prototype regulations had made it even less likely that the Ford GT40 would win races, since it was still subject to an 850 kg (1,870 lb) minimum, but its finest hour would come at Le Mans ...

Brian Redman was signed up to drive with Jo Siffert on a regular basis, and theirs was undoubtedly the best and fastest partnership. Together they won five of the ten races counting towards the 1969 championship, and Siffert won another with Kurt Ahrens in the Porsche 917 at the end of the season. What is more Porsche had sewn-up the World Sports Car Championship before Le Mans, which was back to its usual June date.

The BOAC 500 at Brands Hatch was significant in several ways. It was the first victory for the 908 Spyder, it was the first in which Firestone tyres were raced on a works car, and it was the first time that an Appendix J sports car had lapped quicker than current Formula 1 cars. It was a personal triumph for Siffert, for in qualifying he had his car fitted with Firestones (to whom he was contracted for F1) and claimed pole position at 1 min 28.8 sec. This was 6 sec quicker than he had gone the year before in the 907, and 0.9 sec quicker than he had been in Rob Walker's Lotus 49 while winning the British Grand Prix the previous July.

There was a panic before the race as one bank of the dual ignition system refused to work properly, but despite having single-plug ignition throughout the race he was able to tail the Amon/Rodriguez Ferrari for five laps, then go ahead and command the race. The Ferrari dropped back to fourth at the end, delayed a little by a stretched throttle cable, and the winning average of 100.22 mph (161 km/h) was easily a new race record. Second, two laps behind, were Elford and Richard Attwood, and a further two laps behind were Mitter and Udo Schutz.

Ferrari entered two 312Ps at Monza for Chris Amon/Mario Andretti and Pedro Rodriguez/Peter Schetty, and in combat with four longtail 908s they provided one of the finest races in memory — for the first two hours, at any rate. The banked section of track was in use for the last time, forming only part of the lap as the combined road section was used as well, and time and again Andretti, Siffert, Rodriguez and Elford exchanged places on each lap. Once, memorably, they fanned out to overtake a Lancia Fulvia going past the pits, almost certainly frightening the driver witless, and averaged 133 mph (214 km/h) for the first hour. Andretti had his tyres changed at the first fuel stop, Siffert had a hole in the windscreen taped over, and the battle continued to the two-hour mark.

Then Andretti handed his car to Amon. The American helicoptered away for an engagement in America, Amon driving another two laps 'with nothing showing on any of the dials' to retire with an exhausted engine. Rodriguez and Schetty had two major tyre failures, the second of which caused the Mexican to crash, and later Elford crashed his 908 due to a tyre failure. At the end it was Siffert and Redman leading the 908 of Herrmann and Ahrens, with Gerhard Koch and Hans-Dieter Dechent third in a 907.

At the Targa Florio, Porsche 908s took the top four places against poor opposition from the 2 litre Alfa Romeo T33 fleet, Gerhard Mitter and Udo Schutz winning that one (it was only the second time, in nine Porsche victories so far, that Germans had crewed the winner).

On then to Spa, where Rodriguez and David Piper provided the main opposition in the works Ferrari 312P. Siffert was quickest in practice driving the debutant 917 model, but chose to

drive his 908 in the race, and he and Redman were the only drivers who could keep pace with Rodriguez. A minor collision dropped the Mexican back, though he kept the pressure up, and it was Piper's inability to match his pace that enabled Siffert and Redman to win by three and a half minutes. Behind the Ferrari were the 908s of Elford/Ahrens and Stommelen/Herrmann.

*The 'Spyder' version of the 908 was usually entered for events in 1969, and scored a crushing 1–2–3–4 result in the Targa Florio.*

A revised form of bodywork was seen for the first time at the Nürburgring, taller and flatter between the front and rear wheel arches, with low windscreens curving round to protect only the driver and not his mythical passenger, and with other detail changes that improved the drag coefficient by as much as 20 per cent, from 0.70 to 0.576.

Strictly speaking all the 1969 model 908 Spyders were 908/02 models, but as existing cars were updated the 02 number is now taken to refer to the 'Sole' version. It was, straight away, 15 km/h (9 mph) quicker on the long undulating straight at the 'Ring, but it also had less downforce; Jo Siffert crashed one in practice at the South loop, and Elford had a much larger accident at the Flugplatz when his 908/02 took off and landed where it was not intended to. Flaps, pieces of metal attached to the front bodywork at an angle ahead of the wheels, impaired the drag figure but made the car suitably stable, and the race proved to be a Porsche benefit as 908s occupied the top five places in the results, Siffert and Redman again taking the flag with four more on the same lap.

Amon and Rodriguez provided the only worthwhile opposition but their Ferrari suffered from clutch hydraulic trouble from the start, and retired with electrical failure after 29 of 44 laps while still well in among the Porsches. Despite the handicap, Amon posted the fastest lap at 8 min 3.3 sec, an outright record for the Ferrari sports car, but in practice Siffert had claimed pole position at 8 min 0.2 sec. This was a staggering 33 seconds quicker than his time set the year before, when the 908 Coupé was still in its infancy, and five seconds quicker than the outright record set by Jackie Stewart in a Formula 2 Matra.

Porsche could not have been totally confident in tackling Le Mans with four 908s and a pair of new 917 models, and practice was clouded by the CSI's ban on moving aerodynamic devices, following Formula 1 accidents. Team manager Rico Steinemann threatened to withdraw his six cars, but a brave effort by Rolf Stommelen, in a 917 with the flaps in fixed position, led the officials to allow the devices to be admitted, but only for that race; and in complete secrecy, the Porsche factory had decided to withdraw from active competitions for a while, and had reached an agreement with John Wyer and Gulf Oils to represent the company in 1970 and 1971.

For a while the race ran true to form: the 917s made the early running with Siffert close in pursuit with a longtail 908, and the Gulf GT40s made a steady start lying twelfth and fifteenth after the first hour. Ickx had made his personal protest about the 'run and jump in' start procedure, being used for the last time, by

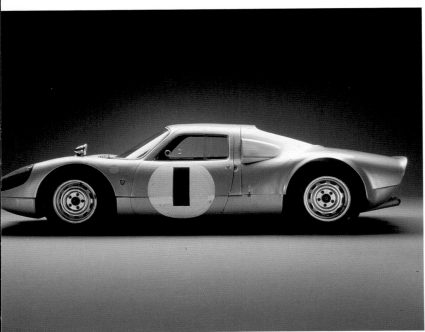

**Above** *Porsche's first 'formula' car was the type 718/2 Formula 2 car built in 1960. Derived from the RS sports cars, the F2 machine was powered by a 1.5 litre, air-cooled, flat-four engine developing 155 bhp.*

**Left** *For a short time, Porsche deserted the tubular spaceframe construction for sports-racing cars, and the 904 appeared in 1964 with a steel platform chassis and with plastic bodywork bonded onto it. As a customer car is was extremely popular, when homologated into the GT class.*

**Above** *Porsche reverted to spaceframe construction with the six-cylinder 906 model, which succeeded the 904 in 1966. It was the forerunner of all the successful sports car designs up to the 936.*

**Right** *The last of the classic 'berg' designs was the 910, in which Gerhard Mitter retained his European Hillclimb Championship title in 1968. A 2 litre, eight-cylinder engine developing 275 bhp was installed in a car weighing as little as 430 kg.*

**Above** *Introduced early in the 1968 season the 908 was rather troublesome at first, but the following year the 908/02 spyder became one of Porsche's most successful models, enabling the company to win the World Championship by June.*

**Left** *Campaigned principally by the JW Automotive Gulf racing team in 1970 and 1971, the Porsche 917 became a legendary success, winning 16 World Championship races in two seasons.*

While the Porsche 917-10 ousted McLaren from the pinnacle of Can-Am racing, it had no competitor in the European Interserie contest. This is Willibert Kauhsen's Bosch – sponsored, 5 litre, normally – aspirated version pictured at the Norisring in June 1971.

walking across the track and deliberately fastening his seat belts. John Woolfe, Porsche's first customer for the 917, had crashed fatally at the White House involving Amon's Ferrari 312P.

After two and a half hours, Siffert and Redman were out of the race, the long tail causing such high temperatures at the rear of the car that the plastic oil pipes around the gearbox melted. Herrmann and Larrousse lost 20 minutes in the pits when a front wheel bearing turned and overheated — a vital stop, as it turned out — and Udo Schutz crashed his 908 in the night, misjudging the Mulsanne kink, being exceptionally lucky to walk away.

On Sunday morning Elford and Attwood were six laps ahead of the Lins/Kauhsen 908, but both cars retired and threw the race wide open. The 917's weak clutch expired, despite having been nursed by the drivers throughout, and the 908 went out with a broken pinion in the differential.

For the last three hours the crowd was treated to a race that had no precedent, the Herrmann/Larrousse 908 duelling with the Ickx/Oliver GT40. Outclassed everywhere else, the GT40 was in its element on the 150 mph (240 km/h) track, and Ickx as usual revelled in the battle. He and Herrmann exchanged the lead regularly, sometimes two or three times in a lap, but in the last hour Herrmann took it easy on braking for the Mulsanne Corner as his brake pad wear indicator was glowing.

That was an electrical fault, though Herrmann did not know it. Ickx should have refuelled one lap before the finish, but caution had to be thrown to the wind. At two minutes to four o'clock Ickx went past the pits with Herrmann in his slipstream, and three and a half minutes later the order was the same. Ickx and Oliver, and the glorious Ford GT40, had beaten Herrmann and Larrousse by 75 metres, officially, the closest result by rival teams in the history of the race.

The factory team was officially disbanded immediately after the race, Dr Porsche realizing that the cost of race car development had left the company with insufficient budgets to run an equally expensive race programme. Porsche Salzburg, owned by Dr Porsche's sister, Louise Piëch, operated the 908s in the last races of the season, and several were sold to private teams including those of Alain de Cadenet, Tony Dean, Karl von Wendt and Gesipa Rivets.

In new colours, Siffert and Redman led a Porsche 908 rout at Watkins Glen, their fifth outright success of the year, and in the final round at the new Österreichring circuit in Austria Siffert gave the 917 its first victory with Kurt Ahrens co-driving. In private hands the 908/02 models would continue to be successful in all parts of the world.

*The lightweight 908/03 made a triumphant debut in the 1970 Targa Florio, Siffert and Redman beating Rodriguez (pictured) and Kinnunen in the leading positions. Like the 909, the 908/03 had its differential behind the gearbox, the driving position being moved forward. This model was built specifically for the Sicilian race, and for the Nürburgring.*

Although the 1970 and 1971 programmes were in the hands of J.W. Automotive, Porsche Salzburg and Martini Racing (a team operated in '71 by Hans-Dieter Dechent) the factory continued a full development programme which included the 908/03, designed specifically for difficult courses such as the Targa Florio, and the Nürburgring where the size and weight of the 917 would be a handicap. In fact the 917 had a much better power:weight ratio of at least 75 bhp/100 kg (600 bhp/800 kg) compared with the 908/03's ratio of 65 bhp/100 kg (360 bhp/550 kg), but the 908 would use far less fuel, would handle much better, have better visibility, and simply be less tiring to drive.

The experience of the 909 'Berg' model was drawn upon to produce the 908/03 including the main elements of the chassis frame, and in particular the situation of the differential behind the gearbox. Again the driver would sit well forward with his feet in front of the axle line, protected by little more than translu-

cent bodywork, and optional items like headlamps were excluded, as the regulations allowed. In 1970 the 908/03 weighed in at 545 kg (1,199 lb), although the figure rose to 565 kg (1,248 lb) in 1971 when wider wheels were fitted, larger fire extinguishers installed, and steel roll-over bars surmounted the alloy chassis. Even the cast-iron brake discs were cross-drilled, it was noted, though not only to save weight since the brakes became more efficient and pad wear was reduced.

The new 908/03s caused quite a sensation when they were presented for the 1970 Targa Florio, three of them for the Gulf/J.W. Automotive team for Jo Siffert/Brian Redman, Pedro Rodriguez/Leo Kinnunen and Richard Attwood/Bjorn Waldegard. Beautifully prepared in Gulf's blue and orange livery, the cars were identified by heart, club and diamond symbols on the front wings. John Wyer's team was consigned to the hills at Cerda, the second refuelling point on the long mountain circuit, and the factory was fully in charge of the operation.

A fourth car was there for training, and a fifth was run by Porsche Salzburg for Vic Elford and Hans Herrmann, after Elford had tested a 917 and found it to be nearly as fast, but too tiring to drive at full speed for more than a couple of laps. For the record, nine were built in the original batch and two more for the 1971 season, most of these finding their way into private hands late in 1971.

A number of 908/02s were in the race, opposed by Nino Vaccarella and Ignazio Giunti in the new Ferrari 512S and a trio of 3 litre V8 powered Alfa Romeo tipo 33/3 models, and it turned out to be one of the most exciting races ever held on the Little Madonie circuit.

The Ferrari was much too big and heavy to be competitive, yet Vaccarella and Giunti drove their hearts out that day. The race started on wet roads, and Elford slid off into retirement with damaged suspension. Larrousse led the first 44-mile lap in a 908/02, unexpectedly, followed by Siffert and Kinnunen, then Gijs van Lennep in another 908/02.

At half distance, amazingly, Vaccarella led the race in the Ferrari, 20 sec ahead of the van Lennep/Hans Laine 908/02. Rodriguez was not enjoying himself and lay third, and five minutes covered the top five cars.

In the second half the Ferrari drivers tired, and Laine, the brilliant young Finn, lost a wheel coming down from Collesano and covered several miles at full speed along the seafront straight, with the front wheel missing. He arrived dramatically in the pits in a shower of sparks, had a new wheel fitted and carried on, still in fourth place.

Redman wrested the lead from Vaccarella and forged ahead to win, while Leo Kinnunen smashed the lap record, leaving it at an all-time mark of 33 min 36 sec as he snatched second place from Giunti on the eleventh and final lap. The Ferrari drivers took a well-earned third position ahead of van Lennep and Laine, with Attwood and Waldegard fifth. It was certainly a triumph for the new 908/03 design and another success, at the Nürburgring, followed.

Laine lost his life during practice, at the wheel of the 908/02, and that marred the event. A nose tab had been knocked off the car but Laine took the car out, at reduced speed, to scrub tyres and bed brake pads for the race. On the long straight the car became airborne over one of the brows and landed upside down, on fire. That tragedy deeply upset his friend and countryman Leo Kinnunen, who asked to be stood down from the race, was refused, then crashed the 908 on his first race lap, so depriving Siffert of a possible victory.

Both Siffert and Rodriguez had practised below 7 min 45 sec, more than 15 sec faster than the 908/02 models had gone 12 months before; they were on Firestone tyres, while the Salzburg entered 908/03s for Elford/Ahrens and Herrmann/Attwood were very little slower, on Goodyears. Since neither of the Ferrari 512S entries could break eight minutes the result seemed to be a formality, but Kinnunen went off almost as soon as he took Siffert's car, which was leading, and Redman ground to a halt with the engine on the point of seizing. The factory had failed to advise Wyer that the 908 had heavy oil consumption, and the tank had not been replenished at quarter-distance!

Two of the oddest reasons for retirement had sidelined the Gulf team, so Elford/Ahrens and Herrmann/Attwood strolled to a 1-2 victory a lap ahead of the cumbersome Ferraris. After that the 908s were dusted off and stored for the following year's races.

Success seemed harder to achieve in 1971. At the Targa Florio the three Alfa Romeos were quickest in practice, all three 908/03 models, now with tall tail fins that helped straight-line stability, having problems. The race turned into a débâcle as Brian Redman and Pedro Rodriguez both crashed on the very first lap, the Englishman being seriously burned on his face when the Porsche caught fire. Elford and Larrousse kept the flag flying in the 908/03 entered by Dechent's Martini & Rossi team, until a puncture led to suspension failure, and the Alfas finished first and second.

Two new 908/03s were made for the Nürburgring, but it turned out that the chassis had been manufactured incorrectly at

a vital point and there was a fundamental weakness. Neither of
the Gulf entries were as fast as they had been the year before,
Ickx taking pole position in his new Ferrari 312PB with Stommelen's Alfa Romeo alongside him on the grid. Sure enough Siffert's car retired early with a broken chassis, so the Swiss partnered Rodriguez who was handicapped by evil handling, for the
same reason and they counted themselves lucky to be placed
second.

Fortune favoured Porsche again though, Ickx retiring with a
cracked cylinder head, his car having overheated from the start,
and Stommelen's engine failed. Elford and Ahrens won the race
for the Martini team, their older 908/03 being trouble-free, and
Rodriguez just held second place from Helmuth Marko's Martini 908/03 by dint of weaving all the way along the straight (he
said it was the chassis, of course).

The 908/03 models were then sold to private teams, most
notably to Reinhold Joest, although 100 kg (220 lb) of ballast

*Not a factory product, the
908/03 turbo enjoyed
success in 1975–76.
Herbert Müller and Leo
Kinnunen drove this car to
third place at the
Nürburgring in 1975.*

had to be added since the minimum weight of 650 kg (1,430 lb) was restored. The principal advantage had been taken away, so the formula was of no interest to Porsche, but even at 650 kg (1,430 lb) the reliable cars could still feature in the results. Joest finished second at Monza in 1972, a wet race that was in his favour, was third at Le Mans in a 908/02, and continued to win the 1973 Kyalami 9-Hours.

In 1974 the factory developed the 2,142 cc turbocharged 6-cylinder, 911-based engine rated at 490-520 bhp, and in 1975 Joest, and Van Lennep/Müller (the latter driving for Dr Dannesburger, and sponsored by Martini) were favoured with these engines for further development. The cars, very unofficially dubbed '908/04' models, were rebodied with Can-Am (917/10) type bodywork and were real hybrids, but they performed usefully in World Championship and Interserie races.

The last World Championship victory recorded by a 908/03 (or '908/04') was at the Nürburgring in 1976, when Reinhold Joest won the first sports car race under new regulations. The new 936 model, the development of the 908, fell back with a stretched throttle cable while the Renault-Alpines collided at the second corner!

When the unsuspecting CSI, sporting branch of the FIA, reduced the homologation requirement for sports cars to 25, instead of 50, they did it to help Lola, McLaren and any other second-league manufacturer who might like to use American V8 engines of 5 litre capacity. They played straight into the hands of Porsche and Ferrari, who made the 917 and 512 models respectively, and created some of the most exciting sports models ever raced in the classic two-seater events.

Under the direction of Ferdinand Piëch the 917 was prepared in great secrecy during the winter of 1968/69, and the type 917 was shown to an amazed public at the Geneva Show in March. A month later the CSI confirmed that 25 had been inspected, all ready to drive away, and Porsche had started a new chapter.

The chassis was still a tubular spaceframe construction, in aluminium tubes and weighing merely 47 kg (103 lb), though in 1971 a magnesium chassis was made weighing 33 kg (72 lb). Hans Mezger designed a flat-12 engine which was, in simplistic terms, two 911-type 6-cylinder, 2.2 litre engines joined together, with power taken from the centre of the crankshaft. It was, of course, enormously more complex than that, but it was a direct development of the 908's flat-eight (itself from the flat-six) with

*In original form the 917 was similar in appearance to the 907 'langheck', though powered by the new flat-12 engine. Presented in Gulf colours in the summer of 1969, the appearance was quickly changed by the British team.*

identical bore/stroke dimensions of 85 x 66 mm, for a capacity of 4,494 cc. It had a magnesium crankcase, titanium con-rods and weighed 240 kg (528 lb), driving through a Fichtel and Sachs triple-plate clutch and an adaption of the 908's 5-speed gearbox (though often only four forward speeds were used, so that wider gear wheels could be fitted).

The power output was rated conservatively at 520 bhp, enough, Piëch believed, to see the team through its first season, though the power was quickly increased to 540 bhp, then 580 bhp even before the full 5 litre capacity was explored. Although the engine was a little longer than a 908's it was located no further rearwards, so the driver's seat was moved forwards, and as in the 908/03 that followed his feet were ahead of the front wheel axis.

The requirement to build 25 cars before a proper development programme had been completed forced a very difficult decision on Porsche, though it had been foreseen. Any modifications needed would be carried out after the batch had been built, and straight away a major weakness showed up. At Spa, where the 917 raced for the first time, the chassis flexed alarmingly and made it difficult to select gears, even more difficult to keep on the road! Siffert made the fastest practice time but wisely chose to race the 908, so Gerhard Mitter drew the short straw and started the race, retiring after one lap with broken valvegear after the 917 jumped out of gear. Siffert's fastest practice lap had been at an average of 142 mph (228 km/h), and at the Le Mans trials Rolf Stommelen had made a fastest lap at 143 mph (230 km/h), topping 200 mph (321 km/h) on the straight. Clearly the 917 had immense potential, but the regular drivers were remarkably reticent about handling it!

Frank Gardner and David Piper were called in to handle the 917 in its second race, at the Nürburgring, and one hopes they were well paid too. Gardner was colourful in his analysis of the car, after driving a cautious race and finishing eighth, and major modifications were carried out subsequently. The chassis was strengthened torsionally, the gearshift layout was changed to prevent inadvertent selection of second, most of the anti-dive geometry was taken out of the rear suspension, and the rear suspension was heavily revised to reduce the travel and keep the wheels more upright in cornering (as was their custom, Porsche had carried out most of the serious testing at the Nürburgring, where full suspension travel was thought to be beneficial. Wide tyres, 12 in (30 cm) in section at the rear initially and 15 in (38 cm) soon afterwards, negated all the old theories).

It was implied in homologation that Sports category cars

would be offered for sale, and the 917 was offered at a very attractive price, DM 140,000 (then approximately £15,000). John Woolfe, a Briton with experience of Can-Am cars, took delivery of his in time for Le Mans, though David Piper was wiser, perhaps, and waited until further development work had been carried out before accepting the car. Woolfe paid his price in full when he lost control of the 917 at the White House corner on the first lap of the race, fatally injured as the car broke in two.

The two works cars of Elford/Attwood and Stommelen/Ahrens went ahead, control helped a little by the moving tail flaps that the organizers were persuaded to accept. Stommelen's car began smoking as oil seeped from a cam cover gasket, and retired in the night from twenty-third position with clutch failure, but Elford and Attwood were nursing their 917 along, knowing of the transmission's weakness, and were six laps ahead on Sunday morning when the clutch began to slip. Eventually the car would move no more, but the practical experience had been invaluable. With the Ford chicane in place Elford set a new lap record of 3 min 27.2 sec, 3 sec quicker than Dan Gurney's 1966 lap record in the 7 litre Ford.

The season ended at the new Österreichring circuit, Austria, in August, and by this time the Porsche management had decided to withdraw from active competitions. The factory would be represented in future by customers, most notably John Wyer's Gulf Oils sponsored organization, and for the fourth and last racing appearance of the 917 in 1969 the two 917s were entered by Karl von Wendt, for Siffert and Ahrens, and by David Piper for Redman and Attwood.

Siffert and Ahrens won that race, though not without great difficulty, beating Herbert Müller and Jo Bonnier in a Lola Chevrolet, with Piper's car in third place. The 917 did not, yet, look like a certain winner.

Wyer and his engineer, John Horsman, felt that the curvaceous bodywork was the root of continuing handling problems, and immediately after the Austrian race they rigged up a new, rising open-deck tail, with a valley across the engine. The Porsche personnel were horrified, feeling that the 917 would probably lift-off at the front, but Jo Siffert reported that the car was transformed, and proved it by lapping four seconds faster than in the race. The breakthrough had been made, and after that it was a case of refining the package.

A Borg and Beck clutch replaced the German equipment, Firestone tyres replaced Dunlops, the bodywork was further refined, and Girling four-piston caliper brakes replaced ATE equipment. This summary of improvements is merely cursory, but performance took a quantum leap.

John Wyer's Gulf Porsche team was a Slough-based extension of the factory's research and development department, privy to all the new developments and updates, and the driver team for 1970 included Pedro Rodriguez with Leo Kinnunen and Jo Siffert with Brian Redman. In addition, though, and as a surprise to Wyer, the Austrian Porsche Salzburg concern was allocated a pair of 917s which were serviced by the factory's customer department, as were a number of genuine private entries. The Austrian company was owned by Frau Louise Piëch, Dr Porsche's sister and mother of Ferdinand, the technical director, and proved to be better favoured than Wyer might have liked. In 1971 the 'second string' operation was taken up by Hans-Dieter Dechent's team sponsored by Martini & Rossi, and this too was able to challenge the Gulf cars on occasions.

If Porsche's 917 had been designed, developed and produced in record time, Enzo Ferrari was even quicker with his response! In the space of six months, from the March debut of the 917, chief engineer Mauro Forghieri produced the 512S model powered by a 550 bhp, 5 litre V12 engine, in fact a four-valve derivative of the Italian company's existing sports car unit. The stage was set for a golden era in World Championship sports car racing, and a confrontation at Le Mans that reached epic proportions.

At Daytona Mario Andretti put his Ferrari 512S on pole position, ahead of the two Gulf Porsches and the Salzburg entry. It was a good start for Ferrari, but a fated race as all the red cars suffered tyre and suspension problems on the banking and dropped out of contention. Siffert's car lost time too with a distributor problem, but Rodriguez and Kinnunen had a perfect run to beat their team-mates by 372 miles (620 km), with the Ferrari of Andretti, Jacky Ickx and Arturo Merzario in third place.

Ferrari had revenge at Sebring, where the Porsches suffered repeated problems with their front hubs, and Andretti scored a memorable victory in the Ferrari shared with Nino Vaccarella and Ignazio Giunti. Peter Revson and actor Steve McQueen were second in a Porsche 908, and Rodriguez/Kinnunen claimed fourth place.

More than a year went by before the Porsches were defeated again. One of the most memorable races was at Brands Hatch in March 1970, run in extremely wet conditions. Pedro Rodriguez was black-flagged for overtaking a slower car under yellow flags, reprimanded by the clerk of the course, and rejoined the race with such verve that he was in the lead after 20 laps. He and

Kinnunen dominated the 1,000 km event, beating the Salzburg Porsches of Vic Elford/Denny Hulme and Hans Herrmann/Richard Attwood by five laps.

A 4,907 cc version of the flat-12 engine, developing 600 bhp, was prepared for the Monza 1,000 Km, but it developed an oil leak in Siffert's car during practice, and was given to Elford for the race. Here, on Ferrari's home ground, there was a battle royal between the Porsches and the Italian cars. Siffert lost 16 laps with a spin and damaged suspension, but Rodriguez and Kinnunen were in commanding form beating the Ferrari of Chris Amon, Giunti and Vaccarella by a lap.

The 4.9 litre engine was generally available for the Spa 1,000 Km, and there Rodriguez established a new lap record for the scenic road course at 3 min 16.5 sec, an average of 160.55 mph (258.33 km/h). This was a full 14 sec inside the existing record, and although the Mexican driver had to retire with a broken gearbox Siffert and Redman took the flag ahead of the Ickx/Surtees Ferrari.

On then to Le Mans, where eight Porsche 917s were ranged against 11 Ferrari 512s. The Gulf team preferred the short 'Kurz' (K specification) tails for better downforce and handling but Elford and Ahrens, in the Salzburg team, were allocated the factory's longtail (L specification) bodywork designed for higher speeds on the Mulsanne Straight. Predominantly wet weather suggested that the short tails would be a better choice — the drivers certainly felt more secure in the conditions — but Rodriguez went out in the night with a broken distributor drive and Siffert over-revved his engine; Mike Hailwood crashed the third Gulf car, and Wyer was denied his hat-trick of victories.

No fewer than four fancied Ferraris were eliminated in one accident when Reine Wisell slowed, unable to see through his smeared windscreen, and started a chain reaction that involved Clay Regazzoni, Mike Parkes and Derek Bell. Bell's car, in fact, was not bodily damaged but the engine was damaged in the mêlée, and such was the rate of attrition that only seven cars were classified at the finish.

Vitally, it was Porsche's maiden victory in the 24-Hour race, achieved by Hans Herrmann and Richard Attwood in a kurz-tailed Porsche Salzburg 917, ahead of a longtail Martini-sponsored car driven by Willi Kauhsen and Gérard Larrousse; in third place were Rudi Lins and Dr Helmuth Marko in a 908, completing the success story for the Stuttgart firm. As a matter of interest, five of the finishers were Porsches, two were Ferraris in fourth and fifth places.

The Gulf team duly mopped up the last two Championship

races of the season, Rodriguez and Kinnunen beating Siffert/Redman by half a lap at Watkins Glen — with Andretti and Giunti third in their Ferrari — and Siffert/Redman taking the flag at the Österreichring, where Rodriguez retired early with valve failure. In Austria the Porsches faced a stronger Ferrari challenge, Ickx and Giunti handling the lightened and more powerful 512M model, but when Ickx seemed to be in command at the 50-lap mark he slowed with electrical problems, and retired.

The ruling CSI body in Paris decided, after the season closed, that these 5 litre cars had to be banned and announced that in 1972 the championship would be for 3 litre cars only. Ferrari decided to develop the flat-12 312P, while Alfa Romeo continued to develop the T33 V8 model, and both these agile cars would press the Porsches on occasions in 1971. In retrospect 1970 had been the finest season, for the 5 litre Ferraris were seen only in private hands the following season.

The 917s were further developed with full 5 litre engines, at 4,998 cc, and produced 630 bhp. Leo Kinnunen was replaced by Jack Oliver, and Brian Redman emigrated (for a year) to South Africa and was replaced by Derek Bell.

Despite their apparent advantages the Gulf team hardly looked dominant in the first four races of the year; the new Ferrari 312P led at Buenos Aires, until Giunti had a dreadful, fatal acci-

*Two tail fins, for stability at high speed, equipped the winning 917 at Le Mans in 1971. This car also had a lighter, magnesium chassis. Drivers, Gijs van Lennep and Helmuth Marko.*

dent hitting a Matra which had run out of fuel. The JW Automotive Porsches came through that to a 1-2 victory, Siffert and Bell leading Rodriguez and Oliver, with the Alfa Romeos placed third and fourth.

Siffert's car retired at Daytona with an engine failure and Rodriguez's lost 40 minutes having its gearbox rebuilt, fighting back to pass a pair of Ferrari 512 models before the end. Sebring was even worse, Bell running out of fuel and losing 23 laps in Sif-

*The 917–20, a unique car, had wide bodywork styled by the French SERA company in a wind tunnel. The Weissach stylists made their opinion known, and nicknamed the car the 'Schwein'. Joest butchered it.*

fert's car, and Rodriguez getting involved in a time-wasting collision. Elford and Larrousse swept through to take a well-
deserved victory in the Martini Porsche 917 pursued by two Alfa
Romeos, with the Gulf-Porsches fourth and fifth.

Neither was there any success at Brands Hatch, where
Rodriguez went out with a blocked fuel line and Siffert lost time
with a difficult wheel change. This wet race was won by Henri
Pescarolo and Andrea de Adamich, Alfa Romeo's first World
Championship success for 20 years.

The ultra-fast circuits at Monza and Spa saw the Gulf-
Porsches on top form again, with new rear bodywork featuring
longitudinal fins for greater stability. Rodriguez and Oliver won
the Italian race at a record speed of 146.54 mph (235.82 km/h),
ahead of Siffert and Bell who had been delayed by a puncture. At
Spa Siffert and Rodriguez took turns at smashing the lap record,
the Swiss finally establishing it at 162.087 mph (260.08 km/h).
Rodriguez and Oliver finished narrowly ahead of Siffert and Bell
(the two team cars slowing, for once, to team orders!) with
Pescarolo's Alfa Romeo far outpaced in third place.

With reduced Ferrari presence at Le Mans a Porsche victory
seemed more than likely ... but which team would win? The
Gulf team had three cars, the Martini team had two, and there
was an interesting, unique Porsche 917-20 in the field, with
wide, short bodywork designed by the French SERA consultan-
cy, directed by Charles Deutsch. The bodywork was 87 in (230
cm) wide, or 7 in (18 cm) wider than the already buxom 917L,
and Porsche's design studio registered their verdict by nicknam-
ing the model the 'Schwein' and painting it pink, marked with
the cuts of pork. Driven by Willi Kauhsen and Reinhold Joest,
the 917-20 had a relatively large frontal area, but was a good
compromise in high speed and downforce.

Roger Penske's Sunoco Ferrari driven by Mark Donohue and
David Hobbs was the most potent challenger, but it was off form
and retired early with engine trouble. Jose Juncadella and Nino
Vaccarella drove the Escuderia Montjuich Ferrari 512S very effectively, though, and actually led at half distance as the Porsche
teams succumbed to or overcame problems.

Siffert had punctured a tyre and damaged an upright, losing
70 minutes; Rodriguez retired with engine damage after an oil
line split; Attwood and Müller needed to have their gearbox
rebuilt, a 40-minute task that prevented the Gulf team from winning. The cooling fan on Elford's engine spun away, causing the
engine to overheat, and Joest butchered the 917-20 in an accident resulting from poor braking.

Helmuth Marko and Gijs van Lennep moved up the leader

board nicely after a careful start, driving the Martini Porsche built around the experimental magnesium frame. The drivers were not even aware that they had a special, lightweight car and might have been concerned if let in on the secret, but the lead was theirs in the thirteenth hour, when Juncadella's Ferrari broke its gearbox, and they kept it going to the end. The fact that the winning car, entered by a customer team, was experimental indicates the level of support that was being given to Dechent by the factory, a point that was not lost on Wyer.

The last two World Championship races in the 1971 season were poignant. Pedro Rodriguez drove one of his finest sports car races at the Österreichring, making up ground after having the alternator changed, and drove all but 20 minutes of the 1,000 km race. Siffert had retired early with a broken clutch (after starting in third gear by mistake) and for much of the time it seemed that Ickx and Regazzoni would be triumphant in the Ferrari 312P. The pressure from Rodriguez, though, was considerable, catching up on a wet track from three laps deficit, and in the closing stages the Ferrari veered into a guardrail.

Rodriguez won that race against all the odds, but a fortnight later he died after crashing Herbert Müller's Ferrari 512 at the Norisring. His name was synonymous with the Porsche 917, and so too was Jo Siffert's. After conceding victory to the Ronnie Peterson/Andrea de Adamich Alfa Romeo at Watkins Glen, where Siffert and Bell were delayed by a broken throttle linkage, but finished second, the Swiss was killed at Brands Hatch when his BRM went out of control.

Their deaths brought a magnificent era in sports car racing to a close, but for many enthusiasts their deeds in 917s remain as fresh as the days they were accomplished.

The 917 K and L versions won 15 World Sports Car Championship races in total, between 1969 and 1971, and including the 908 model successes Porsche actually won 24 of the 31 championship events in three seasons, easily winning the championships each year. Jo Siffert won 10 races, Rodriguez and Redman eight each. Alfa Romeo won three, the Ford GT40 two, while Lola (T70) and Ferrari (512) won a single championship race apiece.

World Championship racing was strictly governed by the CSI, but in North America a new and exciting sports car series was attracting a lot of attention. The Canadian-American Challenge Cup, always referred to simply as Can-Am, was for 'libre' two-seater racing cars, with very few rules other than those governing safety. Engines could be any size, in true sports car tradition, and McLaren Racing, Lola Cars and Jim Hall's Chaparral concern were right in the thick of it, with GM or Ford stock-block V8s.

The series was tailor-made for the Porsche 917 which, despite lacking a couple of litres in engine capacity, was the only one to have a race-designed engine capable of producing more than 100 bhp/litre. The Porsche + Audi company in California begged Porsche to prepare a car, had Jo Siffert's enthusiastic support, and were after all appealing to a German company which sold a quarter of all its produce to the Californian market. There was only one possible response.

The 917PA was easily made, once the essential chassis development had been carried out. The heavy windscreen was removed, and the roof of course, lowering the factory design to spyder form and saving 55 kg (121 lb) in weight. A larger fuel tank was installed, wider wheels were fitted (the rear rims went up to 15 in (38 cm) width, previewing the modification to the World Championship car), and the brake assembly was lightened.

*The Porsche 917 PA was prepared in 1969 for Jo Siffert to contest the late-season Can-Am races. It still featured side exhausts, and was powered by the 4.5 litre flat-12.*

Siffert gave the 917PA its debut at Mid Ohio in August, a week after winning the Austrian 1,000 Km, and it was immediately clear that the 580 bhp, 4.5 litre engine was giving too much away to the 7 litre 'regulars'. Never mind — Siffert had reliability on his side and finished fourth on his debut run, third at Bridgehampton, fourth at Michigan, fifth at Laguna Seca and fourth in Texas, finishing in fourth place overall in the championship despite competing in only half the events.

Although Porsche was, officially, taking a rest from motor racing, some spyder developments of the improved 917 were built in 1970 and 1971 for European customers to compete in the Interserie championship. Following the CSI's decision to banish the 917 from the World Championship, from 1972, Porsche's management decided to switch its energy and prepare a special version for Can-Am competitions. Development work was speeded up during 1971, and one product, which never raced, was a flat-16 engine with a swept capacity of 6,543 cc. It was rated at 755 bhp, with 530 lb/ft of torque at 6,800 rpm, and would certainly have been a winner.

The flat-16 was put aside, though, because Porsche was increasingly interested in the technique of turbocharging. Supercharging had been popular in the 1920s and 1930s (Prof Ferdinand Porsche, founder of the company, had designed the marvellous Mercedes SSK sports car in the late 1920s), but the shaft-driven supercharger was deemed to be inefficient. Rather, the system of an exhaust-driven turbocharger seemed to be a more promising line of development.

Race engine designers Hans Mezger and Valentin Schäffer tackled the technical problems with enthusiasm. Eberspacher turbines, from the commercial vehicle field, were selected and installed in the exhaust system. The problem was not so much getting them to work properly as making the engine drivable, and controlling the 'lag' between flooring the throttle, speeding the turbines up to 90,000 rpm and getting the engine to respond. Much of their development work concentrated on developing a pressure relief 'dump valve', later known as a wastegate, so that the turbo system could be kept under pressure but any excess could be vented.

The 4.5 litre engine developed 850 bhp, but the 4.9 litre version which followed could develop anything up to 1,000 bhp depending on boost pressure. For the customers, however, the normally-aspirated flat-12 was taken out to 5.4 litres, to produce 660 bhp, and ultimately this 5.4 litre unit was turbocharged for the 1973 season, and in Mark Donohue's Penske Team Sunoco Porsche 917-30 it developed a monumental 1,100 bhp.

It was by far the most powerful engine ever developed for a racing car, a contender that would dominate Can-Am racing even more effectively than the 917 model had ruled World Championships.

Porsche's serious Can-Am challenge was mounted late in the 1971 season, in preparation for 1972, and to this end the 917-10 model was prepared. It was based directly on the 917, with all the updates, but to handle the extra power reinforcement was needed for the aluminium space-frame chassis, bringing its weight up to 60 kg (133 lb) bare. The wheelbase was extended by 16 mm (0.6 in) and a new, heavyweight 4-speed gearbox was developed. Suspension travel was further limited, and notably the bodywork was completely new. With almost unlimited power in prospect, for courses which typically had lots of corners and few decent straights, straight-line speed was much less important than downforce. The bodywork therefore was strikingly different with a concave nose panel, air exit louvres above and behind the wheels, a short rear deck and a huge wing at the back. The brakes were made heavier and stronger too, and Can-Am became synonymous with strength and durability.

*The 917–10 version was successful in the Can-Am series and in the European Interserie championship. Leo Kinnunen, rejected by the Gulf team, was dominant in Europe in 1972 and in 1973.*

Jo Siffert competed in four late-season Can-Am races resulting in two seconds, a third and a fifth, which was very encouraging for 1971, but the Swiss driver was then the tragic victim of a crash at Brands Hatch, killed when his BRM veered off the road, and caught fire. He was deeply mourned, and Porsche had to make new plans.

Mark Donohue, America's leading driver of the era, was chosen to lead the 1972 Can-Am programme, driving a 917-10 entered by Roger Penske. A second car was prepared for George Follmer, and it looked as though McLaren Racing would have their hands full dealing with this challenge.

Loose bodywork caused Donohue's Porsche to become airborne, and loop while practising for the second race at Road Atlanta, and the American was lucky to escape with his life; his worst injury was a wrenched knee which kept him out of the cockpit most of the season, but Follmer was able to take over the leadership and win five races, and wrest the championship from Denny Hulme (McLaren). Donohue returned towards the end of the season, and claimed one victory at Edmonton.

*The ultimate racing car, the Porsche 917–30, was driven by Mark Donohue with great success in the 1973 Can-Am championship. The turbocharged flat-12 produced more than 1,000 horsepower with ease.*

The Penske Porsches ran with 5 litre turbo engines in 1972 while most customers ran 5.0 or 5.4 litre normally-aspirated engines, but for 1973 Porsche produced their ultimate weapon, the 5.4 litre turbocharged 917-30 model. A fearsome beast with at least 1,000 bhp available, the final version of the 917 was also the fastest, most powerful racing car ever constructed. It had, for instance, twice as much power as a contemporary 3 litre Formula 1 car and could shatter their records wherever comparisons were possible.

The 917-30 had a magnesium chassis based on that which won at Le Mans in 1971, though strengthened, and the wheelbase was extended by 6.5 in (16.7 cm), the rear bodywork by a remarkable 22 in (56.4 cm). Patient testing had shown that the maximum speed would rise dramatically, from 214 mph to 240 mph (344 to 386 km/h), and since there was nowhere that the top speed could be exploited designer Helmuth Flegl had the leeway to increase the downforce by a considerable margin. Those who drove the car commented that merely releasing the throttle felt like a fierce brake application, and braking almost stood the car on its nose.

Donohue lost the opening rounds of the 1973 season by default, having a minor collision in the first race and a fuel leak in the second, but from then on the combination was completely invincible. He won at Watkins Glen in July, a marvellous 'double-header' programme which included the six-hour World Sports Car round, and then swept through Mid-Ohio, Elkhart Lake, Edmonton, Laguna Seca and Riverside to dominate the points table.

Motor racing had never seen a car like this before, but the era ran out rapidly as the Middle East war produced a legacy of fuel shortages. By the year's end there were queues at the petrol stations, motor sports would become very unfashionable for a couple of seasons, and the organizing SCCA club hastily changed the rule book, introducing a restriction on the amount of fuel that could be used. The Porsches, certainly, were effectively eliminated, and Can-Am racing declined rapidly.

In Europe, though, the equivalent Interserie Challenge survived another two seasons. Leo Kinnunen, driving Antti Aarnio Wihuri's Porsches, had been very successful in 1971, 1972 and 1973, while in '74 and '75 the title was claimed by Herbert Müller. The 917's last successes, however, were recorded in 1975 by the Australian, Tim Schenken, in a 917-10 owned by Georg Loos.

Designed as the successor to the 356 model, the 911 continued the tradition of providing the factory, and countless customers, with sporting successes. The 911 was first shown in Frankfurt in September 1963 and went into production a year later, powered by the now very familiar flat-six engine. At first it had 2-litre capacity and developed 130 bhp, and as soon as the 911 was homologated Porsche employees Herbert Linge and Peter Falk drove it in the 1965 Monte Carlo Rally, finishing in fifth place overall and second, to the 904, in the Grand Touring class. It was a very snowy event in which Eugen Bohringer finished second in the totally unsuitable 904 model, and Porsche's board was, needless to say, extremely satisfied with the result.

The factory concentrated heavily on developing the 904 and its successors for circuit racing, but found time to wring a little more power out of the 911, achieving around 160 bhp with Weber carburettors instead of Solex, re-profiling the camshafts and fitting a free-flow exhaust system. Six-inch wide wheels replaced $4\frac{1}{2}$J rims to put more rubber on the road, and a lot of work was done to improve the wayward handling traits of the early examples.

With assistance from the Zuffenhausen factory Gunther Klass was able to win the 1966 European Grand Touring Rally Championship in a 911, winning the German Rally outright and win-

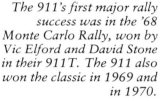

*The 911's first major rally success was in the '68 Monte Carlo Rally, won by Vic Elford and David Stone in their 911T. The 911 also won the classic in 1969 and in 1970.*

ning the GT class in the Alpine Rally, and in September 1966 the long-awaited 911S version was announced with 160 bhp in standard form.

The factory ran its own rally programme in 1967 contracting Vic Elford and co-driver David Stone to drive the works 911T. Further development of the engine took the power up to 210 bhp, and the car soon became a regular winner: a class win on the Monte Carlo Rally was followed by outright wins on the German, Tulip and Geneva Rallies, while Sobieslaw Zasada won the Polish Rally.

In 1967 Porsche also produced the 911R, but did not homologate it due to limited numbers. The 'R' stood for racing, of course, and the intended power unit was the twin-camshaft type 916, as fitted to the 906 racing car, developing 230 bhp. It was highly inflexible, though, and the 'standard' 210 bhp engine was generally installed.

The 911R's chief virtue was its light weight, pared down to 800 kg (1,760 lb), instead of around 1,100 kg (2.420 lb), by stripping out the interior, fitting glass-fibre doors and lids and installing lightweight glass, or plastic, for the windows. The prototype 911R was taken to Monza and run flat-out for four days and nights, capturing 2 litre GT class speed records for 15,000 and 20,000 km, 10,000 miles, 72 and 96 hours. All were at bet-

*A fine day in January 1965, when Eugen Bohringer's 904 and Herbert Linge's newly homologated 911 set off for the Monte Carlo Rally. Conditions were very different in France, heavy snow making the going difficult, but Bohringer achieved a remarkable second place, Linge fifth overall and the GT class winner.*

ween 209 and 210 km/h (approximately 130 mph), and the drivers were Jo Siffert, Rico Steinemann (later to become Porsche's competitions and PR manager), Charles Vögele and Dieter Spoerry.

Porsche had three golden years in rallying in 1968, 1969 and 1970, with innumerable successes. Vic Elford and David Stone won the Monte outright in 1968, followed at 76 seconds by Pauli Toivonen and Martti Tiukkanen in another 911. Bjorn Waldegaard and Lars Helmer won the Swedish Rally brilliantly, Toivonen won the East German, Danube and Geneva Rallies, and Ake Andersson/Lars Svedberg won the Gulf London Rally.

Better was to come in 1969, starting with another 1-2 success in the Monte Carlo Rally. Waldegaard and Lars Helmer led Gérard Larrousse and Jean-Claude Perramond, and a month later Waldegaard made a fine double when he won the Swedish Rally again. The Acropolis Rally, Europe's toughest, went to Toivonen, the Polish to Zasada, the Danube to Poltinger, and the Tour de France to Larrousse/Maurice Gelin.

The 911 was a car for all seasons, accruing a string of track successes too. In 1967 the factory had run a 911S with the new, semi-automatic Sportomatic transmission in the 84-Hour Marathon de la Route and claimed victory with Hans Herr-

*The 911s prepared for the 1968 London-Sydney Marathon were heavily equipped to deal with stray animals (kangaroos were feared especially) and had exhaust pipe extensions enabling the cars to be driven through rivers.*

mann/Jochen Neerpasch/Vic Elford. The Marathon, successor
to the Liège-Rome-Liège marathon (later Spa-Sofia-Liège) was
run exclusively on the Nürburgring circuit where Porsche did
much of their testing anyway, and provided the company with
further testing in the public eye.

In this time the 911 was homologated both as a GT car and as
a Touring car, in slightly different forms, and dominated the
results in both categories. Erwin Kremer/Helmuth
Kelleners/Willi Kauhsen won the 24-Hour saloon/GT race at
Spa in 1968, and the following year the same race was won by
Guy Chasseuil/Claude Ballot-Lena in a 911T. In the World
Championship races the 911 was a reliable GT class winner, and
in the 1971 edition of the Le Mans 24-Hours, for instance, no
fewer than eight of the 13 classified finishers were in 911s!

An increase in capacity to 2.2 litres (actually 2,195 cc) gave
the 911 a new lease of life for 1970, and with twin-plug ignition
a power output of 230 bhp was available for the rally cars. With
a further increase in bore dimensions, the capacity could be
taken to 2,380 cc for racing, and 250 bhp was seen. The 911's
wheelbase had been increased by 2.24 in (5.74 cm) as well, making the car inherently better in the handling department.

Three notable hat-tricks crowned the 1970 season.
Waldegaard and Helmer again won the Monte Carlo Rally, their
second success and Porsche's third. They went on to win the
Swedish Rally for the third time in succession, and later won the
Austrian Alpine Rally. The 84-Hour Marathon de la Route provided Porsche with another hat–trick, this time with a 914
driven by Gérard Larrousse/Claude Haldi/Helmuth Marko,
and the Danube and Spanish Sherry rallies were won by private
entrants in 911s.

Rally successes were becoming harder to achieve all the while,
for Renault-Alpine had produced a new breed of very light,
purpose-built machines with glass-fibre bodywork, a trend later
pursued by Lancia. The rally programme literally ran out of
steam after the 1970 season, although Waldegaard managed second overall on the 1971 RAC Rally and three months later Larrousse claimed second on the Monte. The 911 remained a force
to be reckoned with, even in private hands, and a surprising
postscript to the story is the success of Jean-Pierre Nicolas in the
1978 Monte Carlo Rally, driving a 3 litre 911 entered by the
Almeras brothers.

The factory preferred to concentrate on the Safari Rally, now
the world's most rugged event in which the rather heavy, but
rugged rear-engined 911 could outlast the opposition.
Waldegaard was in action in 1972, 1973, 1974 and again in

1977, the latter year when Martini sponsored a superb two-car team, but success constantly eluded Porsche: Sobieslaw Zasada was second overall in 1972, Waldegaard was second in 1974 and Vic Preston Jr was second in 1977, Waldegaard finishing fourth that time after sustaining shock absorber problems. A new chapter in rallying would come in the 1980s.

The European Grand Touring Car Championship was founded in 1972, and ran through until 1977. Predictably it was the sole property of Porsche's customers, John Fitzpatrick winning the first series for the Kremer brothers, Erwin and Manfred. Despite the odd incursions of cars like the Renault-Alpine and de Tomaso Pantera, anything but a Porsche victory would have been startling, and the customers relied upon 911s at 2.4 litre capacity, and from 1973 upon the newly introduced Carrera 2.7 litre model and its derivatives. When the 934 model picked up the baton in 1976 and 1977 the series died of boredom, but that reflects more upon the lack of opposition than on Porsche's suitability!

The RSR (racing) version was a perfect choice for customers who could rely on upwards of 300 bhp from 2.8 litre capacity. The 1973 season started brilliantly when Peter Gregg and Hurley Haywood won the Daytona 24-Hours outright in their Carrera RSR, which ran as a prototype since homologation had not yet been secured. The same pairing followed-up with success in the Sebring 12-Hours.

Porsche left the Grand Touring category strictly alone, as the domain of customers, and in 1973 concentrated on a wide, wild 'prototype' equipped with a 3 litre engine. In fact it had a new block, a forerunner to the turbo's, with a bore and stroke of 95 x 70.4 mm (capacity 2,994 cc).

The Porsche Carrera RSR 'prototype' developed 315 bhp at 8,000 rpm, and this engine was installed in a lightened chassis turning the scales at 890 kg (1,958 lb). Its wheel arches were grossly flared to accommodate wide wheels, 10.5 in (26.7 cm) width at the front and 14 in (35.9 cm) width at the rear, and 917-type brakes added weight too. The factory car had, of course, plastic doors and lids, and had a full-width aerodynamic spoiler at the rear. The prototype was driven throughout the season by Gijs van Lennep and Herbert Müller, and a second entry was run in Group 4 for purposes of comparison.

Such a car could not compete, in the top class, with proper prototypes such as the Ferrari 312P, Matra MS650/660, Gulf-Mirage and Alfa Romeo Tipo 33, all at around 450 bhp and 600 kg (1,320 lb) ... but again, reliability was an important factor. The prototypes had all failed at Daytona, and few were

**Left** *Three Porsche 911 Carrera RSR models, with 2,806 cc engines, were run at Le Mans in 1973. Heavily outclassed by the Matra prototype which took the top three positions, two Carreras were placed fourth and eighth. This one, driven by Joest and Haldi, ran out of fuel!*

**Below** *Turbocharging, on a 2.1 litre flat-six, raised the power dramatically to over 500 bhp, and the wide-arched, heavily 'winged' prototype of Müller (pictured) and van Lennep ran to second place overall … lacking fourth gear.*

seen at the Targa Florio, a special event for Porsche. In Sicily, in May, van Lennep and Müller drove their 911 RSR prototype to outright victory, Porsche's 11th on the island since 1956, followed by the Lancia Stratos of Sandro Munari and Jean–Claude Andruet.

The 'proto' ran very reliably to fourth place at Le Mans but was demonstrably outclassed in the classic 1,000 km races, eventually claiming third place in the world championship behind Matra and Ferrari.

For 1974 the Carrera RSR was offered to customers as a full 3 litre model, developing 330 bhp reliably, and maintained Porsche's dominance of the GT class. It could accelerate from rest to 62 mph (100 km/h) in 5.4 sec, to 125 mph (200 km/h) in 21.5 sec, and had a top speed of 155 mph (250 km/h). Its equipment included twin-plug cylinder heads, type 917 brakes, competition wheels and tyres, a limited slip differential, and a large rear wing; its homologated weight was 900 kg (1,980 lb).

Porsche's competitions department had a new project in hand, the development of the turbocharged version of the flat-six. Early in 1974 it seemed likely that a new set of regulations would be introduced the following year for 'silhouette' cars, like production cars in appearance but with unlimited power potential. Turbocharging, highly developed on the Can-Am cars, would be

*With bodywork modifications the Carrera RSR 3.0 dominated the European GT Championship in 1974 and in 1975, Georg Loos (car pictured at the Nürburgring) and the Kremer brothers being leading entrants.*

Porsche's route, and chairman Dr Ernst Fuhrmann was, in any case, committed to developing production based models.

The new regulations did not come into effect until January 1976, as it turned out, so Porsche had plenty of time to prepare. In 1974 the 911 Carrera turbo had to run to the existing 3-litre limit, and with a 1.4 equivalency applied to turbocharged engines the nominal capacity could be no greater than 2,142.8 cc ... with a bore x stroke of 83 x 66 mm the turbo engine was 2,142 cc — near enough! A single KKK turbocharger (manufactured by Eberspacher) was installed on the six-cylinder engine, still with fan-driven air cooling, and the power output rose to between 420 and 500 horsepower, depending on how much boost was applied. The aerodynamic rear wing was even larger in size, now dominating the 911's appearance, and the weight was pruned to 820 kg (1,804 lb). The bodywork was still lighter, the fuel tank was moved from the front to the rear passenger area in order to improve race-long handling, and an aluminium structure replaced the sheet steel pontoons that carried the engine, transmission and rear suspension. Notably, the torsion bar suspension was thrown away, and replaced by titanium coil springs.

The first appearance of the 911 Carrera turbo was at the Le Mans trials in March, where two cars showed signs of

*Even in standard form the 911 Carrera RSR 3.0 models were much in evidence in racing. This one, entered by Jean Egretaud, was placed fourteenth at Le Mans in 1974.*

overheating, and sustained failures in their 5-speed gearboxes. Larger air intercoolers were made up, to lower the temperature of the compressed air and make the engines run cooler, and at Monza a month later van Lennep and Müller ran without problems to fifth place overall.

The car (usually one was entered) was reliable during the season finishing third at Spa, sixth at the Nürburgring, second at Le Mans, sixth at the Österreichring, second at Watkins Glen, seventh at the Paul Ricard circuit and fifth at Brands Hatch. The Le Mans result was particularly interesting, because the fancied Matra team suffered a spate of problems and on Sunday morning Henri Pescarolo and Gérard Larrousse lost an hour having their (Porsche designed) gearbox rebuilt. Müller and van Lennep closed to one lap behind but the Matra rejoined the race at full speed, then it was the Porsche's turn to lose fourth gear, causing it to slow down and cruise along to second place.

Now Porsche had learned all they needed to know about endurance racing with turbocharged engines, and prepared no cars for the 1975 season. The 911 Turbo road car was produced for the Paris Show in October 1974, and was produced in sufficient quantity for it to be the base for the 934 and 935 competitions cars that would race in 1976.

These cars, and the 936, are described in subsequent sections, and there was little to report on the 911's competitions development until 1983. Rothmans, Porsche's sponsors on the track, were keen to switch from Opels in rallying and Porsche prepared a special batch of 20 911 SC RS models for an 'evolution' homologation. The 3 litre engine, without a turbocharger, was uprated to 255 bhp initially and to 290 bhp towards the end of 1984, while the weight was reduced to 960 kg (2,112 lb) by using aluminium for the doors, front and rear lids, front wings and front and rear bumpers.

This was the basis for the winner of the 1984 Paris-Dakar Raid, in the hands of René Metge, with a 4-wd system installed, but the main programme was led by Henri Toivonen, son of the former Porsche exponent Pauli. With Ian Grindrod, Toivonen won the Ypres 24-Hours Rally, the Milles Pistes, and Costa Smeralda and the Madeira rallies, finishing runner-up in the European Rally Championship. But for a back injury which put Toivonen out of the series for a while he might well have won the championship. Saeed al Hajri and John Spiller dominated the Middle East Rally Championship in a similar Porsche, and the programme concluded with a two-car outing on the 1984 RAC Rally, in which Roger Clark finished eleventh and Al Hajri seventeenth.

The Volkswagen-Porsche 914/6 was something of a hybrid and is not well remembered at Zuffenhausen. A joint stock company was set up by Volkswagen and Porsche in the late 1960s, based at Ludwigsburg, to produce lower cost sports cars, and Porsche naturally looked after the total design. The 914/4 was powered by VW's 1.7 litre 4-cylinder engine, and was produced in high volume — it was particularly popular in the States — while the 914/6 was powered by Porsche's 2 litre 6-cylinder engine developing 110 bhp. Trouble was, the 911 model was at the same time equipped with the 2.2 litre version and offered higher performance, albeit at higher cost.

The 914's design turned the engine around, placing it ahead of the rear wheels with the gearbox overslung, and the cabin was strictly a two-seater. Although Porsche's management was fairly lukewarm about the project from day one they decided to give it a decent baptism, and the 914/6 was first entered in the 84-Hour Marathon de la Route. All three cars had 911S specification engines, developing 160 bhp, but ran with various stages of chassis development, two of them for instance having larger brake calipers from the 908 racing car, wider wheels, larger fuel tanks and some glass-fibre bodywork.

*The Porsche 914/6 had a short competitions life, and this one driven by Guy Chasseuil/Claude Ballot-Lena had the distinction of being sixth, of seven cars classified in the miserably wet edition of Le Mans in 1970.*

The Marathon, greatly emasculated by that time, was really a high-speed regularity run. With complete reliability, which was taken for granted, the three crossed the line in formation more than 30 laps ahead of a BMW 2002.

Mistakenly, as many people believed, a full team was then entered for the 1971 Monte Carlo Rally, which had been won by the 911 model for the past three years. Perhaps management feared the lightweight Renault-Alpines too greatly, but the drivers Waldegaard, Ake Andersson and Larrousse had difficulty in coming to terms with the 914/6. They felt it was underpowered, and as such was difficult to drive in conditions where 'tail-hanging' would have been advantageous.

Larrousse retired with a broken clutch, Andersson with a broken differential, but Waldegaard gave his best effort as usual and finished a very close third to two French cars, two minutes behind Ove Andersson's Renault-Alpine. He was moved to say that he felt he would have won the rally in a 911.

Sales of the 6-cylinder model slipped disastrously in 1971, falling to a mere 357 cars, and Porsche lost interest completely. Early in 1972 technical director Ferdinand Piëch prepared prototype versions with 2.4 litre engines, unofficially 916 models, and for his own entertainment drove around in a 914 powered by a 3 litre 908 engine (another was built for Dr Ferry Porsche).

Even these powers of persuasion did not work, and the 914/6 project was irrevocably cancelled in 1972. A year later Porsche bought up VW's 50 per cent shareholding in the Ludwigsburg company, and proceeded with the development of the EA425 for VW-Audi. It was the 914 replacement and in 1975 Porsche took a controlling interest in it and launched the car as the Porsche 924.

**Above** *Supplementing the Gulf team, Hans-Dieter Dechent ran the 917 model in 1971 with backing from Martini and Rossi. The 'kurz' (short tail) version is illustrated; the Martini team achieved a famous victory at Le Mans with a similar car.*

**Left** *The world's most powerful racing car, in 1973, was the 917-30 raced by Mark Donohue in the Can-Am championship. The 5.4 litre, twin-turbo engine developed up to 1,100 bhp, and helped him to six consecutive victories.*

**Above** *The science of turbocharging was switched to the 911 production car in 1974, the 911 Carrera RSR turbo powered by a 2.1 litre flat-six developing 500 bhp.*

**Right** *Although the 911 Carrera RSR turbo was far heavier than its 1974 contemporary sports-racing prototypes it was more reliable, and even reached second place overall at Le Mans.*

**Above** *Experience with the 911 RSR Turbo in 1974 prepared the way for the Porsche 935, another outstandingly successful competitions model from the marque.*

*This is the Mass/Ickx car winning its second race, at Vallelunga, Italy, in 1976.*

**Left** *The 936 model was a late entry from Porsche for the 1976 season, but soundly beat the Renault team in every encounter. The 1977 version (illustrated) repeated the Le Mans success, but was not campaigned in other races.*

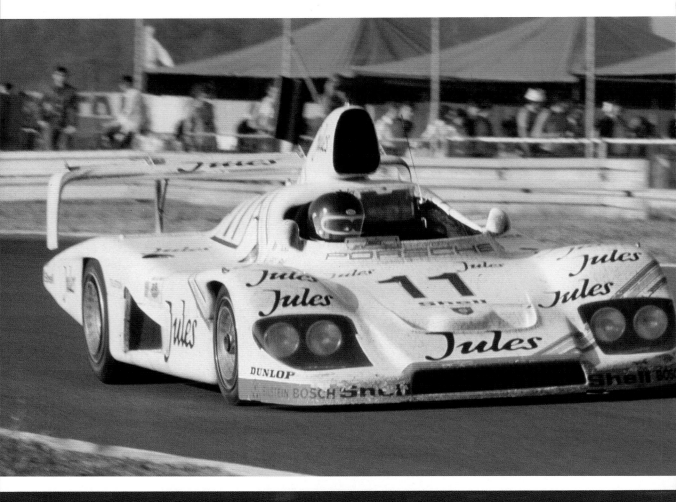

During 1975, preparation for the new Appendix J regulations advanced on three fronts. A successor would be needed for the 911 Carrera RSR, since twin-plug cylinder heads would be barred from the Group 4 Grand Touring Category, and because turbocharging was *de rigueur* in the current programme it was decided to adapt the road-going 911 Turbo (type 930) model for racing.

The Group 5 car prepared for the World Championship for Manufacturers would be known as the 935, and a late addition to the programme was a sports car prepared for the Group 6 World Sports Car Championship, appropriately the 936.

With the 1.4 equivalency factor applied, for turbo or supercharging, the 2,994 cc nominal capacity of the 934 rose to 4,190 cc for which a minimum weight of 1,175 kg (2,585 lb) was applied. This was only 20 kg (44 lb) less than the road-going model weighed anyway, and was achieved easily by stripping the interior, removing the sound-proofing and installing the mandatory roll cage and fire extinguisher. Even the windows remained electrically operated, although air conditioning and in-car entertainment were removed.

Big brakes from the 917 racing car were installed, but the suspension remained pure torsion bar all round. Engine preparation retained the Bosch K-Jetronic injection but the 2.1 litre turbo version's high profile camshafts were adopted and the boost was increased to 1.3 atmospheres (bar, as the Germans phrase it), or 19 lb.

At the start of the programme the engine developed 480 bhp, nearly double the standard model's 260 bhp, and to reduce engine temperatures a new type of intercooler, or interchanger, was adopted, water cooled like a normal engine radiator. Two

*Left In 1981, Jacky Ickx and Derek Bell achieved a perfect Le Mans victory in the 936 model, and broke the distance record. The 2.65 litre engine had twin turbochargers and developed 620 bhp.*

*Below left Porsche's 956 model was the first to feature a 'ground effect' aluminium monocoque, clothed with carbon fibre bodywork. It continued the company's run of championship victories with ease.*

*Porsche's first turbocharged 'customer car' for competitions was the 934 model produced in 1976 and immediately unbeatable. Water cooling for the intercooler was a feature of 934, the radiator mounted in the nose.*

*The 934 model gave good service until 1982, when Richard Cleare and Tony Dron won the GT class at Le Mans. Ultimately their engine delivered 650 bhp.*

water radiators were fitted at the front of the car, either side of the oil cooler, and the water intercooler was both smaller than the air-air unit and more efficient, lowering the charge air temperature by 100°C.

A total of 30 cars was built and sold prior to the 1976 season, priced at DM 97,000 (around £20,000) each, and many appeared regularly in the European Grand Touring Car Championship, which had its own series of races, and in the World Championship GT class. Suffice to say that the Dutchman, Toine Hezemans, won five of the seven qualifying rounds in the 934 entered by Georg Loos (Bob Wollek and 'Tambauto' won the other two, in 934s) while in America George Follmer won the SCCA Trans-Am Championship in a similar car.

Most serious competitors found more than 500 bhp for the 1977 season, and ultimately a 934 campaigned by Richard Cleare was said to produce 650 bhp, though it had a healthy appetite for driveshafts. Private owners regularly chased the 935 teams in World Championship events, and in the States the 934 model completely dominated the SCCA Trans-Am Championship, won by Peter Gregg, and Gregg/Wollek won the World Championship Mosport 6-Hour race outright.

Le Mans, in 1979, was a high point for both the 934 and 935, for at the end of a horribly wet race in which most of the fancied Group 6 cars retired, 935s claimed the top three places and a 934 car was fourth overall, driven by Angelo Pallavicini, Herbert Müller and Marco Vanoli.

The World Championship for Manufacturers (or Makes, depending on translation from French) was introduced on 1 January, 1976 and made a fresh start in endurance racing. The whole rule-book was rewritten, ostensibly to change the emphasis of racing and eliminate the 3 litre sports car 'prototypes' which were, in fact, not prototypes at all but two-seat Grand Prix cars. At a late hour the sports cars were given a separate World Championship, but the major series was for *manufacturers* such as Porsche, Ford, General Motors, BMW, Lancia and anyone else who cared to join in.

The cars would be production based, and would retain the silhouette of the original vehicle, which had to be homologated in series. Power units would have to retain standard blocks, but just about everything else was free, including supercharging or turbocharging.

Porsche had already demonstrated the potential of the 911 Carrera RSR turbo, and had produced and homologated the

*The 935 model won the World Championship for Makes for Porsche in 1976, though the need to change the intercooler caused problems. The 2.8 litre turbo engine gave 590 bhp. A year later, with twin turbocharging and other modifications, the power was increased to 630 bhp.*

911 Turbo model. No one could blame the Stuttgart company for its thorough preparation, but it was so apparent to potential rivals that Porsche was ready to dominate the series that only BMW made any plans to participate, and their effort was not whole-hearted.

The Automobile Club de l'Ouest precipitated the problem by opening the Le Mans 24-Hour race to both Groups 5 and 6, and seemed not to mind losing their championship status, feeling that Group 4 and 5 cars would not be sufficiently attractive to the public. Renault-Alpine chose to concentrate only on Group 6, and Porsche seemingly had a clear run in the Group 5 Makes championship.

Without a ceiling on engine capacities in Group 5 Porsche had no need to run at 2.1 litres, and chose instead a nominal capacity of 2,850 cc, or 3,990 cc with the 1.4 factor applied. At 4 litres the car would have a minimum weight target of 970 kg (2,134 lb) (achieved from the start) and could run with rear tyres not wider than 14 in (36 cm). That was a problem, since the '74 turbo had run with 17 in (44 cm) rear tyre widths, but was alleviated by going up to 19 in (49 cm) diameter rear wheels and enlarging the contact area on the road, the footprint as it is called.

*Potentially, the 935 was virtually as fast as the 936 in the first season, as Rolf Stommelen proved by making the third quickest time in practice at Le Mans. In the race he and Manfred Schurti were badly delayed by ignition problems.*

The 935's construction was similar to that of the '74 model including the rear spaceframe, fully coil-sprung suspension and type 917 brakes, but the 930's heavy duty 4-speed gearbox was incorporated transmitting power through titanium driveshafts; the limited slip differential was fully locked, a system which seemed to benefit drivability and lap times, and enabled the car to reach the pits if a driveshaft failed.

The more bulky air-air intercooler was retained for the 935, but Porsche was soon in trouble with the scrutineers, those at Vallelunga (the second round, in fact) feeling that the high engine cover contradicted the silhouette rule. In Paris the CSI agreed, and gave Porsche just six weeks to resume a 'normal' shape. This involved changing the intercooler system to water-air, a smaller system seen on the 934. It was not a straightforward conversion by any means, and threatened Porsche's chances of taking the main title.

The 935 used Bosch mechanical fuel injection, rather more suitable then for racing than the 934's K-Jetronic system, and with a single KKK turbocharger developed 590 bhp initially. It was said that it would accelerate from rest to 200 km/h (124 mph) in 8.2 sec, though this depended on gearing, and at Le Mans the factory car was timed at 336 km/h (209 mph).

Jacky Ickx and Jochen Mass won the first two races comfortably in Italy, despite the scrutineering problem, but ran into difficulties at the third, at Silverstone, when Ickx burned the clutch out at the start. Standing starts were going out of fashion anyway, and that particular exercise was not repeated, but John Fitzpatrick and Tom Walkinshaw sped to victory in a BMW 3.5 CSL.

BMW had produced a most fearsome car for Ronnie Peterson and Gunnar Nilsson, a turbocharged CSL believed to render well over 700 bhp. Despite its newness it made the front row of the grid and created a magnificent impression as it headed the field ... until its gearbox broke, as confidently predicted.

The modified version of the 935 was prepared for the Nürburgring in May, but development had been rushed and the engine really was not ready. Rolf Stommelen and Manfred Schurti were the nominated drivers and they had to cope with serious throttle lag — despite which they made pole position with a time 8 sec faster than Bob Wollek in a converted 934/5 — and then commanded the race until the distributor arm broke. There were apparently serious vibrations in the engine on part throttle, and a similar problem affecting the throttle shafts stopped three Porsches at the Österreichring in June. Two more victories for BMW, and the Munich company looked poised to snatch the title from Porsche, if the 935 failed again.

With their reputation in danger, to say nothing of the vast cost of development, Porsche's engineers went right through the systems again prior to the Watkins Glen race in July, and were still rig-testing when two cars were air-freighted to the States. The preparation had been thorough and the two cars were reliable, though Mass and Ickx were delayed by a lengthy pit stop due to worn-out rear brake pads. Stommelen and Schurti headed two more Porsches at the finish and BMW claimed fourth place, virtually forfeiting the title.

BMW wheeled out the turbo Coupé again for the season's finale at Dijon, and Peterson planted it on pole position a full 0.5 sec quicker than the Ickx/Mass Porsche. Peterson, the talented and popular Swede, led the race for 40 minutes in a spectacular display, until the rear axle failed, and Ickx/Mass then had a clear run to head four more Porsches in the results.

BMW withdrew from the contest at the end of the season leaving the Porsche factory, and its customers, virtually unopposed: in 1977 the 935s claimed first and second places in every round, and only twice failed to claim third place as well, so that leaves little to say about the series. The factory concentrated on a twin-turbo version of the flat-six, each KKK unit smaller but faster in throttle response, and raised the power to 630 bhp. At the end of the season a batch of 15 such cars was built for customers.

The Porsche 935/2 'Baby' was an interesting diversion in 1977, produced in eight weeks to contest the 2 litre category at the Norisring. BMW and Ford were regular contestants in this division, and to create new interest Dr Fuhrmann ordered the preparation of a class contender, to be driven at the Norisring by Jacky Ickx. The engine capacity was reduced to 1,425 cc by cutting the bore x stroke to 71 x 60 mm (1,995 cc with the 1.4 factor) and the turbocharged unit's power was a very healthy 370 bhp. By eliminating everything not needed for a sprint race the weight was reduced to 750 kg (1,650 lb). The 'Baby' was certainly quick enough, but on a hot day Ickx suffered heat exhaustion and had to retire — there was no heat insulation, and no air going through the car.

He drove the car again at the Hockenheimring, in a race supporting the German Grand Prix, starting from pole position and almost lapping the field before the finish. That was the entire career of the 935/2, which now remains in Porsche's museum.

The 935/78 was another car with a very short though interesting career. Team manager Ing Norbert Singer was instructed to produce an ultimate 935 for selected races in 1978, and designed a model so long and curvaceous that it was dubbed

**Left and below**  *The Group 5 regulations were tested to the limit by the 935/78 model, with streamlined bodywork designed for high speed work at Le Mans. The power unit was a 3.2 litre 'six' with water–cooled, four-valve cylinder heads. The 935/78 won its debut race at Silverstone, but was delayed by ignition problems at Le Mans.*

'Moby Dick'. It was lower because the floor was dropped to sill level, took full advantage of the somewhat relaxed 'silhouette' regulation, and was powered by a new version of the flat-six. This had water-cooled cylinder heads (the cylinder barrels remained air-cooled) allowing the use of four valves per cylinder, and higher engine speeds.

'Moby Dick' went into a higher class, the engine having a nominal capacity of 3,213 cc (4,498 cc with turbocharging), and had to weigh 1,030 kg (2,266 lb). That was fairly unimportant since this power unit developed 750 bhp, at least 100 bhp more than before, and in the higher class it could run with wider wheels which improved the handling.

Mass and Ickx demoralized the opposition at Silverstone on the car's debut, winning by seven clear laps, and at Le Mans Rolf Stommelen and Manfred Schurti drove it as a back-up to the factory's three 936 entries.

Although the 935/78 had the speed to win the race outright, lapping nine seconds quicker than the standard model, at 3 min 30.9 sec, with a maximum speed of 222 mph (357 km/h), it misbehaved for much of the time with a misfiring engine and

*Between 1979 and 1984, when factory interest in the 935 model had waned, specialists prepared their own examples, sometimes retaining nothing more than the powertrain and the windscreen. Preston Henn's 935, illustrated, was second at Daytona in 1984, driven by A.J.Foyt, Bob Wollek and Derek Bell.*

never showed its pace properly, finishing in eighth place. For once the Renault-Alpine team showed Porsche the way home, but the 935's *tour de force* was to come a year later.

The 1979 edition of Le Mans was a miserable affair for most people, run largely in wet conditions and marked by mass retirements among the Group 6 sports car teams. Porsche's own 936 entries were sidelined, and out of the gloom at the finish came a trio of 935s, led by the Kremer Racing K3 special driven by Klaus Ludwig and the American brothers, Don and Bill Whittington. In their wake were Rolf Stommelen, Dick Barbour and film star Paul Newman in a more standard 935.

The Kremer brothers, based in Cologne, produced a very successful 'special' in the K3, which borrowed some ideas from the 'Moby Dick' project, and Reinhold Joest was another who produced his own version. Ultimately little of the original 911 Turbo remained but the windscreen, and the 935 continued its service life very successfully in America in the 1980s, until the 962 model became available in 1984. The 935's tally includes 38 World Championship for Makes victories in the 1976-1981 era, and 91 major successes in American SCCA and IMSA series.

One of Porsche's most successful racing cars came about almost by accident, because the CSI was determined to make the World Championship for Manufacturers the prestige series from 1976 onwards. As mentioned, the Le Mans organizers preferred the Group 6 type sports cars and the CSI decided, in 1975, to introduce a subsidiary World Sports Car Championship, which suited Renault perfectly.

Porsche's management could see that the Group 6 cars would take major honours at Le Mans so, despite having allocated their budget to the 934/935 developments, they found more money to prepare the 936. This model depended heavily on the old 908 chassis technique, which served private teams well with turbocharged engines in 1975. Porsche claimed consistently that the 936 was a new design, with the 2,142 cc turbocharged engine producing 520 bhp initially at 8,000 rpm. Since the minimum weight was 700 kg (1,540 lb), rather than 550 kg (1,210 lb) achieved by the 908, the type 917 5-speed gearbox could be adopted along with the 917's brakes, and the open bodywork was reminiscent of the 917-30's.

The go-ahead for the 936 project was given in September 1975, and in February the still-secret car was given its first run at the Ricard circuit in France ... painted matt black, on the orders of Dr Fuhrmann, to avoid creating much interest.

Renault had prepared well for the series, running two Alpine-developed Group 6 cars powered by turbocharged V6 racing

*The 936 model, raced between 1976 and 1981, became a classic straight away. It won the Le Mans 24-Hours in 1976 (Jacky Ickx/Gijs van Lennep), and all but the opening round of the new World Sportscar Championship. (Photo shows van Lennep at Le Mans.)*

engines, and even in February had little idea that Porsche would be challenging them. Interest was keen when the two makes met at the Nürburgring for the opening round, in April, when Rolf Stommelen handled the new 936 (still painted black, though now with Martini sponsorship).

Patrick Depailler was on pole position in his Renault with Stommelen alongside and Jean-Pierre Jabouille on the next row. Depailler made a bad start, seeing Jabouille forge into the lead, and made one of racing's classic errors entering the second corner of the race, at the north turn. Depailler braked late on the greasy surface, locked up and took Jabouille off the road, both French cars stopping inextricably by the catch fencing.

Depailler was later punished by Renault, having to forfeit the second race of the season, his error having given Porsche a clear run. Stommelen did not win, as it happened, losing power when the throttle cable stretched, but into the breach stepped Reinhold Joest, whose turbocharged 908/03 won the 300 km race with ease. Hezemans was second in the new 934 model, though ineligible for points, and a 2 litre Lola-BMW was third.

Renault had a wretched season, their two cars consistently beaten by the singleton Martini-Porsche 936 handled variously by Ickx, Mass and Stommelen. The cars were very evenly matched, Renault capturing four pole positions in seven outings, but a combination of poor teamwork and bad luck gave the 936 the advantage every time they met.

Although Le Mans was outside the championship, that was the big prize for the 1976 season, and rather strangely Renault entered only one car for Jabouille, Patrick Tambay and José Dolhem. It was fastest in practice but retired on Saturday evening with a holed piston, Ickx and Gijs van Lennep by then being securely in the lead. The second 936 driven by Reinhold Joest and Jürgen Barth was running comfortably in second place on Sunday morning but was then delayed by damaged camshaft rocker arms, and retired later with a broken gearbox input shaft; that was the only 936 retirement of the whole season.

Ickx's 936 had a minor setback on Sunday afternoon when an exhaust pipe fractured, robbing the engine of turbo boost, but at the finish the Belgian-Dutch driving alliance had a lead of 11 laps over the Cosworth DFV powered Mirage of Jean-Louis Lafosse/François Migault. It was Porsche's third Le Mans victory, and the third for Ickx.

Independently, Porsche and Renault decided to concentrate their Gp6 efforts on Le Mans in 1977, the German manufacturer having a full commitment to the Group 5 championship. The 936/77 engine, like the 935's, was equipped with two KKK tur-

*In 1977 the 936 model repeated its triumph at Le Mans, despite holing a piston 45 minutes from the end. Barth, pictured, nursed the car round for two more laps.*

bochargers and the power rose to 540 bhp. Narrower front track, and body modifications, lowered the 936's frontal area and enabled it to run about 15 mph (24 km/h) faster on the long Mulsanne Straight.

Renault entered three cars for the contest, Porsche two, and the pendulum swung to France when Ickx's car retired early with a broken connecting rod in the engine, while Henri Pescarolo was driving. Ickx switched to the second car driven by Hurley Haywood and Jürgen Barth, already delayed 29 minutes by a faulty fuel injection pump.

When Ickx took over, the 936 lay nine laps behind the Renaults in fifteenth place, but the Belgian drove an inspired race throughout the night, consistently below the lap record, to haul the Porsche up to second place by morning. The Jean-Pierre Jabouille/Derek Bell Renault was still a long way ahead, perhaps half an hour in real time, but pulled up with a broken piston, a fate that also dealt with the pursuing Depailler/Laffite Renault.

Injecting still more drama into the last hour, the Porsche 'lost' a piston 45 minutes from the end, though luckily at the Ford chicane. Haywood went straight into the pits where the plug was taken out, isolating the dud cylinder, and Barth had plenty of time to drive the last two laps of the race — another historic victory for Porsche.

In a similar programme, Renault and Porsche met again at Le Mans in 1978. Both teams prepared intensively, Renault running no fewer than four cars in slightly different configurations, Porsche three. Two of these had the latest water-cooled cylinder heads, with four valves per cylinder, and now developed 580 bhp, while the third car, entered for safety, had the 1977 specification and was driven by Peter Gregg, Hurley Haywood and Jürgen Barth.

Porsche seemed to be ill-fated, for Ickx stopped at the end of the first lap with poor throttle return, and the car he shared with Pescarolo lost an hour in the evening when the fifth gear pinion broke. At that, the Belgian moved over to share the Bob Wollek/Jochen Mass car, Mass switching to Pescarolo's, which he crashed after 13 hours of racing. Life could sometimes get complicated for the score-keepers!

Later on Sunday morning the Wollek/Ickx 936 spent 37 minutes in the pits having its fifth gear mended, and they had to settle for second place five laps behind the winning Renault-Alpine driven by Didier Pironi/Jean-Pierre Jaussaud. The

*Following the second success of the 936 at Le Mans (and Porsche's fourth in total) the car was given a 'civic reception' on returning to Stuttgart. Jacky Ickx, the team's idol, is at the wheel.*

936/77 finished in third place, and the huge French crowd went home extremely happy.

The configuration of the 936s was little changed in 1979, a very laid-back season for Porsche, and new livery of Essex Petroleum did not seem to bring any luck. A preliminary run at Silverstone had shown up a potential problem with tyres turning on the rims, and this happened again early in the race causing Brian Redman a bad moment in the fast Dunlop Curve. He avoided an accident, but the radiator was damaged by flailing rubber as he returned to the pits, causing a delay of more than an hour.

Although Ickx did another of his marvellous catch-up performances, he stopped in the night with a broken belt to the fuel injection, and was then disqualified for receiving outside assistance. The sister car driven by Wollek and Haywood was badly delayed by a persistent misfire, much like the 935/78's the year before, but this time the engine was stricken and the works team was eliminated. There was a Porsche victory, though, achieved by Kremer Racing's 935.

Porsche did not enter its top-drawer cars in 1980, concentrating unwisely on the 924 Carrera GT programme, but Reinhold Joest was lent a works car and invited Ickx to share it with him. They seemed to have a very good chance of winning, matched against Jean Rondeau's team of Cosworth V8 powered

*Left New bodywork made the 936 even faster at Le Mans in 1978, and the 24-valve engine was more powerful at 580 bhp. Delayed in the early stages, the Porsche team was beaten by Renault-Alpine on this occasion.*

*Far left A special version of the 936? Reinhold Joest's entry at Le Mans in 1980 was said to have been built at Abtsteinach, but was in fact out of the back door at Weissach. Joest and Ickx were second after repairing the troublesome 5-speed gearbox.*

*Left In its final form, the 936 was powered by the 2.65 litre flat-six engine in 1981, driving through a 'Can-Am' 4-speed gearbox. Ickx and Bell won the Le Mans 24-Hours at record speed.*

cars, but had to settle for second place after coping with a failure of fifth gear.

The glorious finale for the 936 model was at Le Mans in 1981 when two substantially revised cars were prepared for Ickx/Bell and Mass/Haywood/Vern Schuppan. Porsche had a new managing director now, Peter Schutz, who gave the Weissach engineers a free hand in preparing the winner and, taking advantage of the relaxation of the 3 litre top limit, they installed an adaptation of the 2.6 litre turbocharged 'Indy' engine, with four valves per cylinder, developing 620 bhp. It was extremely fast, and reliable, too, using the old 4-speed, heavyweight Can-Am gearbox.

Porsche was fortunate in that all the problems visited one car, though Jochen Mass might not agree. He had to cope with a broken spark plug, a broken clutch and a defective fuel pump in his struggle to twelfth place overall, while Ickx and Bell had a textbook run, losing not a minute for the unforeseen. They smashed the distance record, and Ickx became the most successful driver in the history of the event with five victories.

Traditionally selling more than half its production in the United States, Porsche keeps a close watch on the American competitions scene. In 1979, weary of the World Championship for Makes, Dr Ernst Fuhrmann and Dipl Ing Helmuth Bott reached an agreement with the Interscope team to prepare a car for the Indianapolis 500 mile race, though it was also intended that Danny Ongais should compete in other USAC or CART races.

The P6B was the first single-seater to wear the Porsche crest since the Grand Prix cars of 1962, and the chassis design was a joint effort by Porsche's own Weissach team, led by Helmuth Flegl, and Ted Field's Interscope organization. The chassis was built in America and did not, therefore, carry a Porsche design number.

Porsche was much more involved with the power unit, a development of the familiar 911-based flat-six, prepared by Valentin Schäffer under the direction of Hans Mezger. With a bore and stroke of 95.7 x 66.0 mm the capacity was 2,650 cc, the maximum permitted. The mandatory methanol fuel has such fine cooling properties that the power absorbing fan could be

*This Porsche, the P6B 'Indy', never raced. Jointly developed by Porsche and Interscope, the P6B fell foul of the USAC rule-makers in 1980.*

dispensed with, though a large intercooler was needed between the KKK turbocharger and the Bosch fuel injection. In common with the current 2.1 and 2.8 litre Groups 5/6 cars, the Indy engine had four valves per cylinder and could run to 9,000 rpm, at which speed — ideally — it should develop 630 bhp.

'Ideally' is a critical word, because Porsche and Interscope became involved in politics between USAC, organizers of the Indy 500, and the Championship Auto Racing Teams (CART) organization which was set up, by entrants, virtually in opposition. Their sets of rules were different in some respects, notably in the amount of turbo boost pressure that would be allowed.

Porsche proceeded with the Indy project during the winter of 1979/80 with the verbal assurance that the 6-cylinder engine could run with 14.7 lb boost pressure, with which it could achieve a competitive 630 bhp. When the Indy regulations were published in January 1980 the figure had been lowered to 13.23 lb, at which the engine would develop 570 bhp, but Porsche continued with the development.

Finally, in March, USAC informed Porsche that the permitted boost pressure would be 11.76 lb, at which the engine would develop little more than 500 bhp. Tests were carried out, but the car was neither fast enough nor particularly reliable, and the Porsche-Interscope Indy project was abandoned a few weeks before the Memorial Day race.

Although the Indy project was ill-fated, the 2.65 litre engine development was transferred to the sports car programme, enabling Porsche to win the 1981 Le Mans 24-Hour race at record speed, and then formed the basis for the omnipotent 956/962C Group C cars. In calmer times, Porsche returned to the American single-seater series late in 1987, in preparation for the 1988 season.

The decision to develop the 924 Turbo model was more surprising in retrospect, because Porsche had its own four-cylinder engine under development and this was raced for the first time in June 1981. Later, Prof Bott speaks ill of the VW-Audi-based 2 litre engine as a basis for competitions, but chairman Dr Ernst Fuhrmann was determined to give the 924 model a boost and the 924 Carrera GT model was introduced at the Frankfurt Show in September 1979.

The KKK turbocharger was moved across to the left side of the engine (as would happen later with the 944 Turbo model) where it was cooler; an intercooler was installed and the engine developed 210 bhp, giving it a performance on a par with the

*A team of three 924 Carrera GTR models was prepared for Le Mans in 1980 and this one, driven by Jürgen Barth and Manfred Schurti, surprised and delighted the factory by finishing in sixth place.*

911's. The intention of running a three-car team at Le Mans was settled, and in October Dip Ing Norbert Singer got on with the job of developing the 924 Carrera GT as a basis for Group 4 racing, as well as IMSA GTO and SCCA.

The 924 chassis was substantially lightened to 930 kg (2,046 lb), stiffened with an integral roll cage, and the torsion bar suspension was replaced by titanium coil springs. The GTR model had the 935's centre-lock wheels, and brakes from the 936.

The three cars that raced at Le Mans developed 310 bhp, which was barely enough for them to qualify. They reached 280 km/h (174 mph) on the straight and lapped the Sarthe track in 4 min 7 sec, lining up at the rear of the 55-car grid, which was not a customary position for Porsche! Back at Weissach were two 936 models which might easily have won the event outright.

To emphasize the low-key programme the 924s were driven by 'national' teams: Jürgen Barth and Manfred Schurti for Germany, Peter Gregg and Al Holbert for America and Derek Bell, Tony Dron and Andy Rouse for Britain. Gregg, though, was involved in a road accident before qualifying so Bell transferred to the American car, driving with Holbert for the first time. Subsequently, they would have far more success together.

Slow as they were, the 924s were gaining on reliability and at midnight they lay in tenth, fourteenth and fifteenth positions. Barth lost half an hour in the night when a hare crossed the road in front of him, damaging the water radiator, but on Sunday morning the trio held sixth, seventh and eighth places which looked very respectable.

The promise was not entirely fulfilled, for mid-morning Holbert's engine burned out an exhaust valve, losing compression on one cylinder, and shortly afterwards the same thing happened to the Dron/Rouse car. Both slowed considerably, while the mixture was richened on Barth's car and he ran through to the end without difficulty. He and Schurti claimed sixth place overall, while the other two staggered to the line in twelfth and thirteenth places.

A few replicas of the Le Mans cars were sold to European and American customers, and in 1981 they developed as much as 375 bhp, but reliability was not one of their outstanding characteristics and the factory's interest had already turned to a special version which raced at Le Mans in 1981.

On the entry form the car was a Porsche 924 GTP, but in reality it was a prototype of the 944 model which was about to be announced. Replacing the VW-Audi 2 litre engine was the 2,479 cc, all-aluminium Porsche 4-cylinder engine which, with a single

**Facing page** *Following on from the 924 GTR programme, Porsche's own 944 engine was installed in a chassis for Le Mans in 1981. It had a four-valve cylinder head and was turbocharged, developing 420 bhp. It was driven to seventh place by Jürgen Barth and Walter Rohrl.*

KKK turbocharger, developed 420 bhp. Previewing future developments the Porsche engine had four valves per cylinder and Bosch Motronic engine management, a very clean and efficient system. The chassis and body were almost identical to the 924 Carrera GTR's, but the brake discs were larger in diameter.

Testing at the Ricard circuit did not go smoothly at all, with repeated failures of the cylinder head gasket. It seemed that 1.3 bar (18.2 lb) of boost pressure and 450 bhp was more than the open-deck block could cope with, and there was no time to endurance test the GTP at 1.1 bar (15.4 lb) before the race.

Rally ace Walter Röhrl was enlisted to drive the car (he handled Porsche 911s and 924 Carrera GTRs in some European rallies that year, when his Mercedes programme foundered) with Jürgen Barth, and perhaps they surprised themselves by having a perfectly trouble-free run to seventh place overall, while at the head of the field Jacky Ickx and Derek Bell won with equally conspicuous ease.

It was an excellent weekend for Porsche, and the 924 GTP also won a prize for spending less time in the pits than any other competitor. A week later the Porsche 944 was announced, and it had, already, won its spurs.

Every now and again motor racing produces a classic design, and the Porsche 956 was such a car. Soon after the outstanding success of the 936 model at Le Mans in 1981 the new chairman, Peter W. Schutz, gave the go-ahead to prepare a new car designed for the Group C regulations that would come into force in 1982, the basis of which would be the 2.65 litre, flat-six, twin turbocharged engine.

In its first season the engine was equipped with Bosch mechanical fuel injection and developed 620 bhp, though in 1983 the factory adopted the full Motronic system and, with greater fuel efficiency, was able to raise the power to 640 bhp.

The crux of the new regulations was to run a 1,000 km (620 mile) race on 600 litres (132 gallons) of fuel, which would be measured into the tank at a rate of 50 litres (11 gallons) per minute. There was no limit on engine size, configuration, or the power that could be developed: so long as the car did 4.7 miles per gallon (60 litres/100 km) it was raceworthy.

At Weissach, chassis expert Horst Reitter designed the aluminium monocoque to the limit of the regulations, which allowed the car to be a maximum of 480 cm (189 in) in length, 200 cm (79 in) wide and 110 cm (43 in) high. A flat metal plate

*If the 936 was one of Porsche's most successful racing cars, the 956 was a worthy successor. It won the Group C class at Silverstone on its debut, and became the outright winner at Le Mans, Spa, Fuji and Brands Hatch, collecting titles for Porsche and Jacky Ickx.*

*The 956 model, current from 1982 to 1986, was Porsche's first monocoque design, by Horst Reitter. It needed little modification from one season to the next. The engine is tilted upwards towards the rear, to make space for the ground effect venturi.*

of 100 x 80 cm (39 x 31 in) had to be placed underneath the floor in order to restrict the 'ground effects' though venturi were installed on either side of the engine. The minimum weight allowed was 800 kg (1,764 lb), but the 956 started life at 840 and was 'dieted' to 815 kg (1,797 lb) in 1983.

The water and oil radiators, and intercoolers, were all placed at the sides of the car so that a clean, sharp nose profile could be obtained, and the shape of the 956 was carefully refined in Porsche's scale wind tunnel at Weissach. Through the official radar trap at Hunaudières, on the Mulsanne Straight, the 956s were timed at 370 km/h (230 mph), which was actually no faster than the 5-litre, 620 bhp 917 models went a decade before. The 956, though, carried a large rear wing and had advanced ground effects, which tended to slow the car on the straight but made it far quicker around the corners. Comparisons of lap times are meaningless because Le Mans had undergone two major changes in the meantime.

Early in 1982 a contract was signed bringing the works team major sponsorship from the Rothmans cigarette company, an eminent partnership which brought the two companies considerable success in the next six years. Jacky Ickx and Derek Bell were the lead drivers in 1982, and they gave the 956 model its debut at Silverstone in May.

Two factors worked against Porsche at Silverstone. Because there would not be enough cars to sustain the new formula in its first year FISA (as the ruling body was now called) admitted Group 6 cars which would not be able to claim points for the

World Championship for Manufacturers, and Lancia (in partnership with Porsche's former sponsor, Martini) upset the ap-
plecart by building a new, lightweight, open sports car powered
by a 1.4 litre turbocharged engine. It was at least as fast as the
Porsche, and the drivers never had to worry about fuel
consumption.

Secondly, the organizing BRDC was allowed to retain the
6-Hour duration, and average speeds were such that Riccardo
Patrese and Michele Alboreto covered 1,132 km (703 miles) in
their Lancia while Ickx and Bell, using only top gear in the last
hour to save fuel, covered 14.7 km (9.13 miles, three laps)
fewer. They did win Group C, of course, a debut victory, but it
was not as stylish a success as Peter Falk's team wished for, and
in subsequent years the British round was strictly limited to
1,000 km (620 miles).

Porsche missed the Nürburgring race later in May to prepare
thoroughly for Le Mans, developing, building and testing three
956s for the epic. Jacky Ickx and Derek Bell shared the lead car,
Jochen Mass and Vern Schuppan the second, and Al Holbert/
Hurley Haywood/Jürgen Barth the third.

Opposition came from a strong Rondeau team, winners in
1980, from Aston Martin Nimrod, Joest 936C, Kremer CK-5,
Ford C-100, Lancia, Sauber and Lola, a very strong field in
theory. One by one, though, the cars in opposition retired or
slowed with mechanical problems and the result was a text-book
success for Porsche: from pole position, Ickx and Bell led all the
way, travelling 74 km (46 miles) further than in the 936 the year

*Triumphant is the only
word to describe the 956
squadron as it lined up for a
1–2–3 finish at Le Mans in
1982. The cars had been
perfectly reliable, and two
broke the previous year's
distance record.*

before. In second place Mass and Schuppan exceeded the previous year's mark by 34 km (21 miles) while Holbert/Haywood/Barth finished third. In the closing laps the Porsches numbers 1, 2 and 3 cruised round in the correct order for a stage-managed finish, heading a pair of Porsche 935s.

There had not been an intention to contest the full World Championship, but with 10 weeks to prepare for the Spa 1,000 Kms the temptation was just too great, and a pair of cars was entered for Ickx/Mass and Bell/Schuppan. They were, again, in dominant form, and development work with Robert Bosch had virtually removed concerns about fuel consumption. Ickx and Mass won the Belgian race, heading Bell and Schuppan by three laps with the Lancia pushed firmly into third place, and a further resounding victory for Ickx and Mass at Fuji, Japan, in October enabled Porsche to win the World Championship for Makes.

One event remained, the Brands Hatch 1,000 Kms counting towards the Drivers' Championship, and Ickx was able to persuade the factory to send a 956 for himself and Bell. If Ickx could beat Patrese's Lancia he would win the title, and the two drivers did, indeed, enjoy a thrilling duel.

Run in heavy rain at first, the race was stopped when the two Ford C-100s collided and spun off, then restarted with Ickx a few seconds ahead of Patrese. As the track dried Bell lost a full lap to the Lancia and held on just too long on unsuitable tyres on instructions from the pits, while the Belgian faced a seemingly impossible task of catching up in the final hour. In gathering dusk he seemed to fly round the Kentish circuit, opening gaps where they hardly existed, overtaking, undertaking — who knew what was happening round the back of the circuit?

At his brilliant best, Ickx had his headlamps blazing in Patrese's mirrors when the chequered flag came out, and Falk prepared to concede defeat. For a minute he forgot the slender advantage of the first heat, and when the times were added together Ickx had won the race, and captured the title, by 4.7 sec! It was a memorable race, a splendid finale to the first Group C season, and confirmed Ickx as a great champion. The 956 was pretty good, too.

In time for the 1983 season Porsche built a dozen 956s for sale to customers. Two went to Japan, one to Preston Henn in America, but the majority were campaigned regularly in Europe by Reinhold Joest, Erwin and Manfred Kremer, Richard Lloyd/Canon Racing, John Fitzpatrick, Walter Brun and Jürgen Lässig/Obermaier Racing. They were all faithful to the 1982 design, and highly competitive, and any advantage enjoyed by the factory team that year — Jacky Ickx with Jochen Mass, and

Derek Bell with Stefan Bellof — was down to weight-shedding, and to the use of Bosch Motronic engine management.

Indicating just how effective these cars could be, Reinhold Joest dealt the factory team a dig in the ribs by winning the opening round of the season, at Monza. Bob Wollek, who felt himself to be a 'factory reject', and Thierry Boutsen judged their fuel ration to perfection in the 1,000 km race and beat Ickx/Mass by 80 sec, while the fastest lap was set by John Fitzpatrick.

Lancia challenged with a new Group C car, the LC2, powered by an adapted Ferrari 2.6 litre V8, with twin turbochargers. It was certainly quick and offered a token of opposition, since Ford had dropped the C-100 programme, but Italian successes were rare indeed in three seasons. The first, of three, was at Imola in October 1982, a drivers' championship race not attended by the Porsche factory.

By inference, all the others were won by Porsche whose run of successes went on, and on, and on. The works team usually beat the customers although there were rare exceptions, such as John Fitzpatrick's success at Brands Hatch in September 1982. Fitz had Derek Warwick driving with him and, with Goodyear rain tyres working effectively on the streaming track, Warwick almost lapped Ickx before a pace car interlude, and then repeated the medicine when the race speeded up again.

*Winners at Le Mans in 1983, Vern Schuppan, Al Holbert and Hurley Haywood crossed the line only seconds before Jacky Ickx and Derek Bell.*

Le Mans, in June, was another *tour de force* for Porsche, the 956 model taking the top eight places, and tenth. The Lancias tried hard but retired early in the night with engine and turbo

problems, the Rondeaux were by now outclassed, and the only interloper in the top ten was a BMW 6-cylinder powered Sauber driven by Americans.

Again the Rothmans-Porsche team seemed to be heading for a 1-2-3 victory, until Jochen Mass's engine became terminally stricken and ground to a halt around Sunday lunchtime. There was a hectic race on Sunday afternoon between Schuppan/Haywood/Holbert and Ickx/Bell, the Belgian aiming for his record seventh victory. Just for once his legendary luck did not hold, and Schuppan held a slender lead to the flag despite an ailing engine; earlier the left-side door had flown away and, with the radiator airflow spoiled, one bank of the engine overheated. Bell would surely have passed him if another lap had been available.

Ickx again won the drivers' championship, narrowly beating Derek Bell, and to the chagrin of the British driver it was his 1984 team-mate, Stefan Bellof, who seized the title that year after a very fine season.

The year got off to a controversial start when FISA decided not, after all, to reduce the allocation of fuel by 15 per cent (to 510 litres (112 gallons), for a 1,000 km (620 mile) race). The ruling body had engaged in further talks with the American IMSA controlling body to see if the two sets of regulations could be brought together; basically IMSA differed in rejecting the fuel consumption control altogether, preferring a sliding scale of weights and engine sizes to even the competition. It was a curious situation because no one really liked the fuel consumption formula, but it seemed to be the best way of equating performances for manufacturers, as opposed to teams.

In preparation for 1984, both Porsche and Lancia had carried out a good deal of expensive development work (none of which was wasted, of course), and as a mark of protest against FISA's new attitude Porsche withdrew its entries from the Le Mans 24-Hour race. Later in the year FISA and IMSA agreed to continue their separate ways and the lower consumption regulation was introduced for 1985.

The record for 1984 shows that the Rothmans-Porsche team won all the races it entered including Monza, Silverstone, the Nürburgring, Mosport Park, Spa, Fuji and Sandown Park. Bellof won six races including the Imola 1,000 Km, a driver championship race forfeited by the factory, when he drove for Walter Brun.

Without factory representation, Le Mans was won in fine style by Reinhold Joest's 956 entry driven by Klaus Ludwig and Henri Pescarolo, the German entry finishing two laps ahead of

**Left** *In the absence of factory Porsches, Reinhold Joest entered the winning Porsche 956 at Le Mans in 1984. It was driven by Klaus Ludwig and Henri Pescarolo.*

**Left** *A rare double was achieved by Reinhold Joest's team in 1985, winning the Le Mans 24-Hours with the same chassis, number 117, that won the previous year. The drivers, Klaus Ludwig, Paolo Barilla and 'John Winter', beat the works team handsomely.*

*Outwardly like any other Porsche 956, Richard Lloyd's team at Silverstone designed a new chassis in 1984, of honeycomb aluminium construction and with fully adjustable suspension. It was a strong second at Le Mans in 1985, was first at Brands Hatch in July 1986, and, adapted to 962C form in 1987, won the Norisring 200 Mile race.*

Preston Henn's Porsche co-driven by Jean Paul Jr and Jean Rondeau. Then, Porsches merely filled the top seven positions, eighth claimed by Bob Wollek and Alessandro Nannini in a Lancia-Martini.

Reinhold Joest's Porsche 956 team again won at Le Mans in 1985, the same car (chassis 956/117) handled by Ludwig with Paolo Barilla and 'John Winter'. The victory was all the better for Joest because he was up against factory cars, the Rothmans-Porsche team now developing the 962C chassis. The most significant factor in the Rothmans defeat was not the chassis at all, but failure to programme the Motronic management system correctly for the lower consumption required.

The final year of the 956's career was in 1986, after which the chassis would be outside the regulation which stipulated that the pedals must be within the car's wheelbase. Opposition was increasing, from the Silk Cut Jaguar team which won the Silverstone 1,000 Km and from the Kouros Sauber Mercedes team which won at the Nürburgring. In July Richard Lloyd's

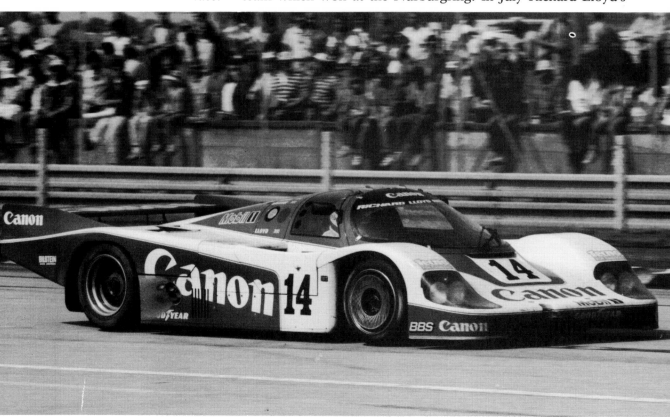

Porsche team won the Brands Hatch 1,000 Km for the second time, but with a different car. Whereas the 1984 success was with a conventional Porsche chassis, handled by Jonathan Palmer and Jan Lammers, the team then developed its own chassis designed by Nigel Stroud, and Bob Wollek and Mauro Baldi drove it to the chequered flag in '86.

Lloyd called it a Porsche 956B, or 956 GTi. Outwardly it was a 'regular' Porsche, and many parts were interchangeable, but the chassis was made of honeycomb aluminium for greater strength and safety, and the suspension was fully adjustable in Formula 1 style. We will count that as a Porsche 956 success, and the last of all was achieved, at Fuji, by Joest's famous 956/117 which ended its career famously.

As a model, the Porsche 956 won 27 World and Driver Championship races between 1982 and 1986, second only to the 935 model which won 38. Add, if you like, 14 World Championship victories for the 962C model between 1985 and the end of the 1987 season, then the full tally is 41 major successes ... and 48 more in IMSA, to August 1988.

With the 956 programme well under way in 1983 Porsche turned its attention to the American IMSA championship, where the 935 model was still valiantly holding the fort. The Americans' unwillingness to adopt FISA's Group C regulations in 1982 had disappointed all the Europeans, not least Porsche and its customers. In one particular respect the 956 was ineligible for the GTP category, since the driver's foot pedal box was ahead of the axis of the front wheels, contrary to IMSA's safety inspired regulation.

The 962 model, which made its debut in the Daytona 24-Hours in January 1984, easily overcame the objection by extending the wheelbase by 2.4 in (6.2 cm) at the front, and placing the axis ahead of the pedals. The bodywork was changed a little at the front, more at the rear since only one turbocharger was permitted, a huge KKK located behind the power unit. Customers could specify their own engine developments, and capacities ranged between 2.8, 3.0 and 3.2 litres, while sliding scale weights ranged from 900 to 940 kg (1,980 to 2.068 lb) (ballast was needed, since the 962 could weigh as little as 870 kg (1,914 lb)).

Mario Andretti and his son, Mike, drove the car in its inaugural race which ended with a broken transmission during the

*Unlike the Group C cars, the 962 IMSA championship model has a single KKK turbocharger located behind the engine, entailing different rear bodywork.*

evening, but the main points had been covered — the 962 handled well and was a leading runner, all that potential customers needed to know. The race was won, incidentally, by the South African Kreepy Krauley team with a Porsche engine in a March 83G chassis. The 935's career was at an end, and had the 962 not been built customers would have deserted the Porsche camp and bought March and Lola chassis, for which a variety of American V8 engines were available.

The power units were, and remain, fully air cooled since the 4-valve heads would entail higher car weights, and Alwin Springer's Andial company was responsible for most preparations. Early customers included Al Holbert, whose Löwenbräu-sponsored outfit was virtually the 'works' team, Bruce Leven, Bob Akin, the BF Goodrich Tire Company, and Preston Henn, and later the legendary A J Foyt, Rob Dyson and John Hotchkis.

Opposition was certainly stronger and healthier than in Europe, though the combined weight and sheer reliability of the Porsche army usually won the day … and the longer the event the better the Porsches became, making the Daytona 24-Hour race their domain. Bob Tullius's Group 44 Jaguar team was a consistent rival until 1987, Ford tried hard with the Probe programme,

*The debut of the longer wheelbase 962 model was at Daytona in January 1984, when it was driven by Mario and Mike Andretti. It retired in the evening with a broken gearbox.*

with Klaus Ludwig as the lead driver, Nissan had a strong presence with Lola chassis entered by Electramotive, and the quickest car of all, often, was the Lola chassis Chevrolet Corvette GTP, with Sarel van der Merwe leading the drivers.

Porsche's IMSA teams won 46 races between June 1984 (Road America, won by Holbert and Derek Bell) and the Del Mar, California, finale to the 1987 season (won by Jochen Mass for Bruce Leven's team), and was beaten only on 11 occasions in three-and-a-half seasons: Randy Lanier's Chevrolet-March won two in the latter part of 1984, the Jaguar XJR-5 gave Porsche their only defeat in 1985 at Road Atlanta, Sarel van der Merwe's Chevrolet GTP won two races in 1986, a season in which Klaus Ludwig won at Laguna Seca in the Ford Probe, Davy Jones and John Andretti won at Watkins Glen in a BMW, and Bob Tullius/Chip Robinson won the Daytona season-closer in the XJR-7. In 1987 the Porsche 962 continued its victory trail, scooping all the successes except Miami (Nissan), and Riverside and Palm Beach (Jaguar XJR-8).

A run of successes particularly worth noting is that achieved by Al Holbert and Derek Bell, who won the Daytona 24-Hours in February 1986, going on to win the Le Mans 24-Hours in June driving the Rothmans-Porsche 962C with Hans Stuck. In 1987 they won the Daytona 24-Hours again, with Chip Robinson and Al Unser Jr, and repeated their success at Le Mans. They and the Porsche 962 model therefore won four consecutive 24-hour races.

For the 1985 season the Porsche factory adopted the 962 chassis, changing the type to 962C with various changes to suit Group C. The factory and customer cars used the four-valve, twin turbo engines of course, developing upwards of 640 horsepower, and a notable feature of the works cars was the fitment of 19 in (49 cm) diameter rear wheels, 16 in (41 cm) in width, allowing space for taller 'ground effect' venturi.

In 1986 and 1987 the factory cars were equipped with 3-litre, fully water-cooled engines, the previously air-cooled cylinder barrels having water jackets, thus disposing of the big cooling fan. These engines were made available to customer teams in the latter part of the 1987 season. Another feature exclusive to the factory was the PDK (Porsche Doppel-Kupplung) semi-automatic, twin-clutch transmission which, although heavier than the usual 5-speed manual, allowed 'stepless' shifting and produced faster lap times.

The adoption of the 962C chassis coincided with the reduced fuel allocation at the start of the 1985 season, and until and including Le Mans this was to give the Rothmans team extraordinary difficulties. The first race, at Mugello, saw the Hans Stuck/Derek Bell entry run out of fuel within sight of the finish, but Jacky Ickx and Jochen Mass were poised to take the chequered flag. Manfred Winkelhock and Marc Surer won the second round at Monza, but that was an unusual race because a gale swept the circuit, felling a large tree across the track! The race was stopped prematurely at the four-hour mark, and no one could imagine what the final result might have been, because so much depended on fuel remaining for the last hour.

The works Porsches looked well beaten at Silverstone, until the leading Lancia dropped out and the Lloyd Canon-Porsche broke an oil line, so Ickx and Mass won again, pursued by Stuck and Bell. Le Mans was certainly not theirs for the taking, the Joest and Lloyd teams having a terrific scrap all the way to the finish followed, at seven laps, by Stuck and Bell.

The micro writing on the Motronic chip was corrected, and in the latter part of the season the works Porsches started winning regularly from the front, not by default. Stuck and Bell won at Hockenheim, a race in which the fuel reservoir in Ickx's pit exploded, resulting in manager Norbert Singer being taken to hospital with nasty burns, and they won again at Mosport, a race marred by the fatal accident of Manfred Winkelhock. The Lancia team then won at Spa, an equally tragic race stopped prematurely by Stefan Bellof's fatal accident in Walter Brun's Porsche. Winning the Brands Hatch 1,000 Km late in the season confirmed Derek Bell and Hans Stuck as joint champion drivers, a long overdue credit to the Englishman.

*Consistently one of the most successful Porsche 962 teams in IMSA was Al Holbert's, sponsored by Löwenbräu. Holbert won the GTP championship in 1985 and in 1986, while in '87 his lead driver Chip Robinson claimed the title.*

*In 1988 Porsche faced a lean time, losing the Daytona 24-Hours to the new Tom Walkinshaw directed Castrol-Jaguar team, and later suffered seven successive defeats handed out by the Electramotive Nissan team. Porsches won only two of the first ten races in 1988.*

**Far left** *The 962C model made its debut at Mugello in 1985, where Ickx and Mass were successful. The wheelbase was extended by 2.4 in (6.2 cm), and 19 in diameter rear wheels were fitted.*

**Below left** *Bell, Stuck and Holbert won the Le Mans 24-Hours in 1986 in the Rothmans-Porsche 962C ... but the factory would not win another World Championship race for 12 months.*

**Left** *The Rothmans-Porsche 962C took Hans Stuck and Derek Bell to a fine World Championship in 1985, and although they tied on points Bell was the sole champion in 1986.*

Bell and Stuck continued their success story in 1986, though the going was getting harder all the time. The PDK transmission was not perfectly reliable, nor did their car handle as well as it should have done with 25 kg (55 lb) of extra weight hung behind the rear wheels, but they were required to use it for most races and won the Monza 360 km 'sprint', an innovation in the calendar. Le Mans though, with a normal transmission, was the highlight of their season, and the opposition mustered two successes, Silk Cut Jaguar at Silverstone and Kouros Sauber Mercedes at the Nürburgring. The German race was remarkable, run in dreadfully wet weather conditions at the start, and flawed by a heavy collision between Stuck and his team-mate, Jochen Mass, in blinding spray.

The works Porsche 962C models were lightened to the 850 kg (1,870 lb) minimum for 1987, and Peter Falk indicated that the last possible developments had been wrung out of the ageing chassis. In contrast, the Tom Walkinshaw-operated Silk Cut

Jaguar team, powered by production based V12 engines, reached a high level of speed and reliability and won eight out of ten races. Their successes were difficult at first, against the works Porsches, but became a dominant feature when the Weissach team withdrew from the series in June. Pressure of work involving the new Indycar, and the Formula 1 programme, led to Porsche's temporary withdrawal.

Again, though, the highlight of the year was victory at Le Mans, achieved this time by Bell, Stuck and Holbert against long odds. Ignition programming was a problem again, due in 1987 to a new regulation requiring the use of low-lead, commercially available fuel, and an hour into the race only one works Porsche remained (Mass's retirement was put down to a water loss, but the customer teams were decimated).

The three Jaguars eventually succumbed, one with an explosive tyre failure, one with a cracked cylinder head, and one with a broken gearbox which was repaired, and on Sunday afternoon Bell, Stuck and Holbert were the relieved winners, by a wide margin from the Primagaz sponsored 962C.

Two weeks later the Britten-Lloyd team won the Norisring 200 Mile race with its unique 962 driven by Jonathan Palmer and Mauro Baldi, both Jaguars having hit problems, but for the remainder of the season the privately run Porsche teams had to wave goodbye to the Coventry cars.

In the space of seven seasons, though, the works Porsches from Weissach had written a new page in the history books. In particular, seven Le Mans victories in succession, between 1981 and 1987, carried the marque past Ferrari as the most successful in 24-hour racing. Three more for the 962, at Daytona, underlined that fact.

**Left** *Only one factory Porsche 962C survived the first hour of the Le Mans race in 1987 but that one, driven again by Bell, Stuck and Holbert, vanquished the Silk Cut Jaguar team.*

**Left** *Throughout 1986 and 1987 Hans Stuck handled a PDK twin-clutch Porsche 962C in the German Supercup series, winning the title in '87. Eventually, the 1987 version proved faster than the normal, 5-speed model.*

A particularly prosperous period of trading in the United States between 1982 and 1986, coupled with heavy reliance on the American market, encouraged Porsche's management to return to the 'Indy' scene. The Formula 1 engine programme undertaken for the TAG company, and McLaren International, was drawing to a close, and Hans Mezger and his assistant Valentin Schäffer had amassed a huge store of knowledge that could be put to good use.

Peter Schutz, chairman of Porsche during 1981-87, was an American with a good feel for that market, and in 1984 he had established a new sales organization, Porsche Cars North America headed by John Cook. Al Holbert was then appointed director of motor sports for North America and in 1987, before the car was built, he signed the Quaker State oil company as the main sponsor for the 1988 programme.

There was new stability in American single-seater racing too, with unequivocal rules established by the CART organization which administered the championship. The Indianapolis 500 is to the series what Le Mans is to the World Championship for

*Porsche returned to the American circus in 1987 with the type 2708 'Indy' car, totally designed at Weissach. It competed in the last two races of the season in preparation for 1988.*

sports cars, so although Porsche's new car was called the 'Indy', it was intended for the whole series.

The 2708 was designed entirely at Weissach, the 2.65 litre V8 engine developed by Mezger and Schäffer, the chassis and bodywork by Horst Reitter. They examined a contemporary March in detail and put it, and their own design, in the new Weissach full-size wind tunnel. The chassis, incidentally, made of honeycomb aluminium and composite materials, was manufactured by the Messerschmitt company in Bavaria.

The engine design broke new ground for Porsche, being the company's first V8 specifically for racing, and with a bore and stroke of 88.2 x 54.2 mm it has a capacity of 2,649.2 cc. The 90° V8 has four valves per cylinder, with twin camshafts on each bank driven by gear wheels. The engine is water-cooled but runs on methanol in accordance with the regulations, and is programmed by Bosch Motronic engine management for injection and ignition.

With a single Garrett turbocharger limited to 48 in (123 cm) of mercury pressure (0.62 bar, or 8.75 lb) the engine develops 750 bhp at 11,200 rpm, though it will run to 11,800 rpm. Although much more powerful than the still-born flat-six Indy engine, which developed 630 bhp at best, it has substantially less torque at 465 Nm (47.4 mkg, or 342 lb/ft) at 8,500 rpm. In 1980, the flat-six developed 57 mkg of torque at 6,400 rpm.

A new 6-speed gearbox was developed for the 2708, which made its debut at Monterey in October 1987, driven by Al Unser Sr. The car was sadly off the pace and retired early with a broken water pump, then failed to qualify for the Miami finale when it was driven by Al Holbert. Critics who did not know Porsche very well were quick to disparage the car, but the Germans had rushed the development programme at almost impossible speed in order to gain race experience at the end of the 1987 season, and then had five months to prepare the 2708 for 1988.

Teo Fabi, the Italian driver, was lured from the Benetton F1 team to develop and drive the Porsche, and before the season began it was decided to concentrate on the March chassis, removing one of the unknown areas. By mid-season, the Porsche-March began to move up the grid, and Helmuth Flegl was brought in to speed up the development.

When the Porsche 959 first appeared, at Frankfurt in September 1983, it was designated the 'Gruppe B' study, indicating that it was regarded as the Stuttgart company's answer to the Audi Quattro rally car. The build of 200 road cars, with a complex four-wheel drive system and extremely advanced mechanical specification, was seriously delayed and was not due to be completed until midway through 1988, and in the meantime a new breed of rally car, models like the Peugeot 205, the Metro 6R4 and the Ford RS 200, changed the face of Group B rallying. They were forest racers, weighing less than 1,000 kg (2,200 lb), and with mid-engine configurations were far more nimble than the 959, and its 961 competitions derivative, could ever hope to be. FISA signalled the end of Group B rally cars in 1986, following the death of Henri Toivonen in a Lancia.

It was already clear, when the 959/961 development programme got under way in 1984, that it was not going to be a serious rally contender. It was, however, ideally suited to rugged prototype events such as the Paris-Dakar Raid, an event which captured the imagination of Jacky Ickx. He persuaded Porsche's management and Rothmans' to support a three-car entry for the event run in January 1984, and that is where the 959's history begins.

*A prototype of the 959 model, the 4-wd 911, won the 1984 Paris-Dakar Raid in the hands of René Metge and Dominique Lemoyne.*

René Metge and Dominique Lemoyne won the event in their
Porsche and Jacky Ickx was sixth, with Claude Brasseur, after
coping with a burned-out wiring loom. Their cars were by no
means the definitive 959s because they competed with normally-
aspirated 3-litre engines, had 5-speed gearboxes and a rudimen-
tary, mechanical four-wheel drive system utilizing an Audi
Quattro differential between the front wheels.

A more definitive version of the 959 was first seen in the 1985
Paris-Dakar Raid, using the cockpit-operated hydraulic torque
splitter which varied the amount of power available to the front
wheels. The three cars were powered by 3.2 litre Carrera
engines, without turbocharging, and developed 230 bhp, but
none of them finished; both Ickx and Mass hit boulders, and
Metge missed a passage control.

In preparation for the 1986 'Raid', two cars were entered for
the Egyptian Rally of the Pharaohs late in 1985. Ickx's car was
the early victim of an engine room fire (the turbochargers set
light to the wiring, and some useful experience was gained) but
Saeed al Hajri, from Qatar, romped through to victory.

The Porsches entered in the 1986 Paris-Dakar Raid were
definitive 959s in most respects, including the 2.8 litre twin-
turbo engines which developed 400 bhp — they were detuned to

*The last official event for
the 959 model was the 1986
Paris-Dakar Raid, won
again by René Metge and
Dominique Lemoyne. The
2.8 litre 'six' had twin
turbochargers, developed
400 bhp, and transmitted
drive to all four wheels via a
new 6-speed gearbox.*

run on poor quality fuel — the complex four-wheel drive system, 6-speed gearboxes and the curvaceous bodywork with faired headlamps and flat tail treatment, with an integral spoiler. They lacked the Westinghouse Wabco anti-lock brake system and the self-levelling hydraulic suspension struts, but seemed to be very sophisticated for the 22 day trans-Saharan adventure.

The 14,000 km (8,700 miles) route was packed with incident for the 487 competitors, Ickx losing time with a holed radiator and more when he became bogged down in treacherous sand. Metge and Lemoyne experienced no serious delays in completing the route, taking victory with Ickx and Brasseur less than two hours behind in second place. Their back-up crew, Roland Kussmaul with Hendrick Unger, were sixth.

Technically the 959 development programme was completed and the cars were not seen again in competitions. Kussmaul, manager of the 961 competitions model development, then turned his attention to the lightweight 4-wd racing car that made its debut at Le Mans six months later. Special lightweight aramid (composite) materials were used for the bodywork and the weight was reduced to 1,150 kg, the minimum for the IMSA GTX category in which the car ran. The engine, capable of producing 680 bhp, was detuned to 640 bhp for reliability.

Driven by René Metge and Claude Ballot-Lena, the 961 ran through to seventh place overall in the 24-Hour race, covering 320 laps at an average of 180.65 km/h (112.27 mph). A burst tyre at speed, which led to a driveshaft failure, was the only technical problem in that outing, but Kussmaul and his team were certainly disappointed that the 961 could lap at no better than 3 min 47 sec, with a top speed of 193 mph (310 km/h) on the straight.

The next appearance of the 961 was at Daytona later in 1986, where the car was handicapped by the need to run on 12 in (30 cm) wide rims. It was not the handling that caused problems but heavy loading on the banking, resulted in the Dunlops overheating and failing. Factory test driver Gunther Steckkonig and Kees Nierop drove an 'underwhelming' race to twenty-fourth place overall, and failed to impress the Americans with the $325,000 (around £210,000) racer.

The 961 appeared only once in 1987, at Le Mans, driven by Metge, Claude Haldi and Kees Nierop. Although the power was up to 680 bhp, Metge's practice time was actually slower than the previous year's, at 3 min 50.8 sec, and the team had a fraught race with driveshaft failures, accident damage, and finally on Sunday morning, a difficult gearshift which prompted Nierop to spin into a barrier, and retire from the race.

The 961's development story may end there, on a low note, but FISA has announced the inauguration of a Grand Touring Car Category (GTC), virtually replacing Group B, in World Championship races from 1989 onwards. Models such as the Porsche 959 and Ferrari F40 will be eligible, but evolutions such as the 961 will not. Whether or not the 959 takes part in any more competitions, it has had a peculiarly chequered career unlike that of any other Porsches built seriously for competitions.

*Rather less successful than the 959 model was the type 961 competitions derivative, seen here at Le Mans in 1987. Due to a recalcitrant gearbox, it crashed.*

# Index